Praise for *Coaching Up!*

"Jordan Fliegel was an outstanding basketball player who became a brilliant coach and entrepreneur. He brought all three skill sets together in founding CoachUp, Inc., which is so masterfully enabling thousands of coaches and players to work together. Now he is offering all of us his original, creative, and eminently implementable ideas in this remarkable book, which will appeal to everyone who coaches or is coached in sports, business, or any other activity."

—**Marc Gerson**, Cofounder and Chairman of Gerson Lehrman Group, Thuzio, United Hatzalah, African Mission Healthcare Foundation, and United Rescue

"Jordan's success as an athlete and entrepreneur can be attributed to his keen understanding of the elements of effective leadership—whether on the court or in the boardroom. *Coaching Up!* is a fantastic read for you if you believe in building genuine relationships with teammates, colleagues, and friends—especially if you want to know how to provide active support and how to inspire success."

—**John Harthorne**, Cofounder and CEO of MassChallenge, a startup-friendly accelerator whose 835 alumni have raised $1.4 billion, generated $575 million, and created 8,500 jobs globally to date

"Jordan Fliegel's insights and guidelines, based on first-hand experience with professional athletes and top-notch coaches, apply equally well to the coaching needed by students, aspiring entrepreneurs, and executives struggling to meet the challenges of development and growth, as well as to those working to succeed on the playing field."

—**Edward Roberts**, Professor, MIT Sloan School of Management, Founder and Chair, MIT Entrepreneurship Center (now the Trust Center for MIT Entrepreneurship)

"*Coaching Up!* soars above the array of books on how to be a good coach or leader by literally practicing what it preaches. In this engagingly written book, Jordan Fliegel addresses his readers directly in a frank, first-person conversation about how inspirational leadership actually works. In doing so, he creates with us exactly the kind of connection he describes as the basis for coaching someone up, i.e., what any writer, coach, executive, or parent aspires to: an authentic and heartening relationship with his or her readers, players, colleagues, or family members."

—**Adele Pressman**, Child Psychiatrist; Assistant Clinical Professor of Psychiatry at Harvard Medical School; Author of Pump Prout: a Little League Novel; and the mother of two Division I athletes

"The way people work has radically changed, and as business leaders we need to evolve our approach to coaching, too. Jordan really gets this and provides actionable guidance for leaders to create the right environment for employee growth and transformation."
—**Brian Halligan**, Cofounder and CEO of HubSpot; Author of *Inbound Marketing: Attract, Engage, and Delight Customers Online*

"Employee coaching is such an important part of a successful company culture. As *Coaching Up!* emphasizes, guidance and transparency are more important than ever. They can be the deciding factors between a mediocre and a remarkable company."
—**Dharmesh Shah**, Cofounder and CTO of HubSpot; Author of *Inbound Marketing: Attract, Engage, and Delight Customers Online*

"In *Coaching Up!* Jordan Fliegel demonstrates how the best coaches build trusting relationships, focus on strengths, and give specific timely guidance for effective action. Vibrant coaching success stories and proven techniques make this book an essential read for all management and life coaches, and for everyone exercising leadership in families and organizations."
—**Joan Bragar**, EdD, Author of *Leading for Results: Five Practices to Use in Your Personal and Professional Life*

"I have always been an overachiever. Growing up in a family in which my mom and dad were married and divorced four times each and I had lived in 17 apartments by the time I was 18, with a lot of violence in the family unit, I was lucky to have sports and some great mentors to guide me toward a better future. Growing up, I did not have tools like the ones found in *Coaching Up!* That's the bad news. The good news is that reading *Coaching Up!* has given me great new tools for leadership and for life. I will use these tools to continue to drive and refocuse my energy, not only for myself, but also for the benefit of my close business, entertainment, and political associates. Congratulations, Jordan."

—**Scott Brown**, former U.S. Senator and
Fox News Contributor

COACHING UP!

COACHING UP!

INSPIRING PEAK PERFORMANCE WHEN IT MATTERS MOST

JORDAN FLIEGEL
with **KATHLEEN LANDIS LANCASTER**

WILEY

This book is for all the fathers who have steadfastly coached me up over the years: my devoted father and best friend, Dorian Fliegel; my terrific stepfather, Michael Keating; my magnificent godfather, Guido Goldman; and my unfailingly supportive honorary father, Elliot Levine; and for my beloved one and only mother, Kathleen Lancaster, who suggested to me some decades back that it might be a good idea to write things down from time to time, and who is still helping me do it.

With all my love,
JLF

Contents

Foreword

I'm thrilled to be writing this foreword to *Coaching Up!*
The fact is, I feel passionate about coaching. To me,
coaching means having the ability to move people from
point A to point B—taking them one step closer to
maximizing who they are and becoming whoever they
want to be. It's an undervalued skill in our society. People
who serve as that kind of catalyst for others are truly
exceptional.

I have a deeply personal reason for appreciating the
impact coaching can have: coaching made me who I am. I
literally wouldn't be where I am in my life without the
people who coached me along the way. I've been
extraordinarily lucky to have worked with some of the
greatest coaches of all time. Each of them has challenged
me, pushed me, and helped me along on my journey. In
fact they personified, each in his own way, the three core
elements of the Coaching Up Model you'll find presented in this book: building an authentic connection,

providing genuine support, and offering concise direction—along with a whole lot more. They made me a better player, a better team member, and a better man.

In the end, my legacy as an athlete isn't how many points I scored or how many charges I took. Looking over my career, I see two seminal achievements: the fact that I was a multiple champion at every level, from Little League to two National Basketball Association (NBA) championships, and the fact that I was always one of my teammates' favorite teammates. Both of those achievements stemmed directly from the brilliant coaching I received along the way.

But before I get into a few of the most valuable ways my coaches connected with me, supported me, and offered me direction, let me tell you a little bit about how my journey began.

In the Beginning . . .

The greatest coach I ever played for, hands down, was my dad, Ed Battier, known to one and all as Big Ed. I grew up in Birmingham, Michigan, in a very sports-oriented family. Sports were just always present; in fact I learned to read from the sports pages of the newspaper. My younger brother, Jeremy, and my dad and I spent a lot of time together watching sports and playing them.

I was so lucky to have a dad who was a part of my journey every step of the way, from an early age. He was my baseball coach every single year, he was my football coach every single year, but he was never my basketball coach. And that's ironic, because he had a storied career playing for his army base's basketball team in Mannheim, Germany, where he was stationed. His claim to fame, which he never let me forget, was that he once scored 50 points in a game. I never scored 50 points in any game, so Big Ed's got one up on me.

But no matter which sports I was playing, and which teams he was coaching, the personal coaching I got from my dad in the front yard never centered on technique. It was never about "You need to hold your elbow at this angle, or you need to have a high knee kick." Instead, what he taught me—what he showed me—was enthusiasm, dedication, and discipline. He was just always present and unfailingly willing to practice. Whenever I said, "Dad, let's play catch," he would always grab his glove and say, "Let's go."

My dad worked at a steel transportation company for 40 years. He hauled steel, warehoused steel. It was the blue-collar mentality, the assembly-line mentality: every day you show up, you punch in, you do what you do; at the end of the day you punch out, you go and have a beer, and you go home to your family. And the next day you get up and do it again.

That's what I call toughness, and discipline, and living a principled life. Today, being a dad myself, I realize how tired he must have been, coming home at the end of the day. But I never once heard him complain about having to go to baseball practice or having to coach the football team, let alone tossing a ball with me. He really was—and still is—an amazing man in that regard.

He was also a very impressive man generally. For one thing, he was the only black guy in the whole town of Birmingham, Michigan. For another, he was huge: big biceps and a hulking presence. Growing up, I thought he was the strongest dad in the world. So he commanded attention immediately. No one *ever* messed with Big Ed. Every team I was on that he coached always gave him immense respect.

In his team coaching and in our casual games and practices at home, he taught me several key lessons that were seminal to my development as an athlete and as a man. Those lessons, which he harped on every day, were the same ones I took with me to the NBA finals in 2013. He constantly talked about, and demanded, hustle, sportsmanship, attitude, communication (also known as chatter), and looking sharp.

Here, in brief, is Big Ed on those five key lessons:

■ *Hustle:* He would never outright yell at his teams to hustle. If he felt that we were loafing, he would shout, "Hey, hey, hey, let's go!" in a booming voice that told everyone to put some pep in their step. It always worked.

- *Sportsmanship:* If you focused on Big Ed right at the end of a game, you would not know whether we won or lost because his reaction was always the same: he would hustle over to the opposing coaches and offer a huge smile, a handshake, and big compliments on the completed game. We learned always to respect our opponent regardless of the outcome.

- *Attitude:* One of the rare times my dad would raise his voice was when he saw somebody get down on a teammate or, even worse, down on himself. He would say, "Come on, Shane, you can do it! Now act like it! You have to believe! Change your attitude." There was no room for negativity on our teams.

- *Communication/chatter:* If you were out in the outfield and you weren't verbally supporting your pitcher and your teammates, if you weren't engaging in chatter on the field, you were going to hear it from Big Ed—and no one wanted to hear it from Big Ed. You always supported each teammate verbally and let him know you had his back. Sports were not a silent activity.

- *Looking sharp:* If you looked sharp, with your shirt tucked in, you were going to play sharp. If you practiced sharp and took batting practice or fielding sharp, you were going to play a sharp game. Everything was about game speed and game focus— amazing habits to build.

These are invaluable lessons that I have carried with me every step of the way.

But the single most important lesson I learned from Big Ed was this: when you're playing a team sport, the team comes first. With him, it was never about individual success. My dad never praised me individually for how many runs I scored or whatever—it was always "*Wow*, how great was our team tonight!"

He's not a man of many words. He never said, "I'm going to teach you the lessons of how to be a great teammate or how to be a champion." But that's exactly what he did teach me. I've learned so much just from being around him, from how he carries himself.

He's the reason I have the legacy I have today, no question about it. Because of his coaching, my aim was always to make every teammate better, from the best players to the thirteenth man on the team, the guy who couldn't hit at all. My dad always taught me that every team member deserves your respect and your support. So that was how I related to my teammates.

When I talk with my childhood buddies who also played with Big Ed, we all marvel at the way he had with all of us. The only time he raised his voice was when one of us was not being a great teammate. That was it. There was never a tirade, ever. There was never a dressing down. Of course, if you didn't hustle up the field, you were going to hear his deep, booming voice—"Hey, hey, hey, let's go!"—which scared the living hell out of you.

But it was done respectfully, and with love. I know that, to this day, all my teammates I grew up playing Little League with would say that Coach Battier—Big Ed—coached with love.

Finding Connection and Support

So, Big Ed gave me my base. After his teaching, I played under a lot of coaches, from childhood up through high school, various camps, college, and the pros. And going in the door, I always respected my coaches. I believed that coaches occupied a position that deserved that respect. I also believed that they deserved my energy, my focus, and the benefit of the doubt, and I gave them all those things.

But my journey wasn't an easy one—far from it. It's pretty obvious, when you're 6 feet tall in sixth grade and 6′4″ in seventh grade and 6′8″ in eighth grade, that you've got the right body type for basketball. But there's so much more to the game than height and athleticism. I've been so fortunate to have just terrific coaches, who've shown me not only the technical and tactical aspects of the game, but the psychological and strategic aspects as well, and who have enhanced every step of my journey. Moreover, they saw the potential in me and had the patience and the foresight to invest their energy in me.

For instance, my Amateur Athletic Union coach, Burk Kozlowksi; my assistant high school coach, Jay Schwartz; and my high school coach, Kurt Keener, all spent an incredible number of hours in the gym with me. I was a total gym rat. I was the equivalent of a Labrador retriever that would keep fetching the ball and fetching the ball till his joints gave out. I was constantly in the gym. And to have my coaches join me there, and come along on the journey because they believed in me . . . that was an unbelievable motivator.

Not only did they help me hone my skills and boost my confidence, but also, thanks to them, I realized that I wasn't alone. And that was amazing. All that effort, all that striving and striving, can be a pretty lonely thing. Plus you're a kid: you can't grasp everything psychologically; you're just trying to get through puberty alive.

I'm pretty sure that every kid that age experiences uncomfortable self-consciousness and some degree of loneliness. In my case, those feelings were exacerbated by the fact that I was always an outlier. For me, the ultimate motivator was always fear. I was scared that I wasn't good enough, that whatever success I had was just a dream, that I'd wake up and I'd be by myself.

The main thing that defined me as an individual was growing up mixed, with a black father and a white mother. At Pembroke Elementary School, my buddy Eddie Toma was the token Hispanic, and I was the token black kid. Everyone else was white. When you're just trying to fit in, that's tough for a kid to digest.

And so, on class picture day, when everyone got a comb, I got a pick. And there I was, an outlier, a foot taller than everybody else and the black kid. And when I went into downtown Detroit to get some competition at basketball, the brothers were saying, "Look at that kid from the suburbs who talks so white; look at him." So no matter where I went, I was always different.

But in the end there was one kind of place where I did fit in: on the local sandlot, on the basketball court, and on the kickball field. I realized at an early age that when I helped people win, they liked me and I did fit in. So for me, winning was a social survival tool. And it wasn't about winning by dazzling everybody else with my skills. It was about winning by helping our team—all of us—feel good and play our best. So that's where I learned it. And that's what my legacy is to this day: I always played, at every level, to make whatever team I was on as good as it could be.

So, that was a seminal period in my life; it shaped me, and I wouldn't change it for anything. It was hard as hell when I went through it, but it galvanized me. And having great guides along at my side, acting as a stabilizing force, a motivating force, and allies—that was invaluable.

The other fundamentally invaluable support I had came from my mother and father. They never, ever put any pressure on me to practice sports or to earn high grades in school. The only thing they ever asked of me

was to do my best at whatever I was doing. I always knew
that they were there for me. They never missed a game I
played in, and they were endlessly willing to drive me all
over the country to various gyms and games and training
opportunities. I always knew I had their absolute support
and love.

With all this support from my family and coaches, and
with my experience on lots of teams, eventually I realized, "Okay, I'm different, but who cares?" I learned to
love being different!

In my senior year of high school, our team—the
Detroit Country Day School Yellowjackets—won the
Class B state championship. I was named Mr. Basketball
for the state of Michigan as well as the Naismith national
High School Player of the Year.

Of course, playing at the college level would be a
whole different game.

Playing for Coach K

So by the time I got to college and played for Coach K
(the Duke University Blue Devils' renowned—and
revered—Coach Mike Krzyzewski), the coaching bar
in my world had been set very high. Coach K had a
lot to live up to. (I think that was a new experience for
him!) And boy, did he ever. If there was one coach who
was up to that task, it was Coach K.

What distinguished Coach K from all the other coaches who tried to recruit me to their college programs was that he didn't promise me a place in the starting lineup, and he didn't dangle before me the potential spoils of victory. Instead, he promised me only one thing: that every day I would have the opportunity to earn playing time. Even before I had committed to Duke, that was his way of challenging me intellectually: "are you mentally tough enough to accept that challenge?"

And earning playing time was not going to be easy. Coach K fostered an unbelievably competitive environment. Our practices were much tougher than our games. I was the Naismith national player of the year that year, but we also had the number two player and the number four player in the country in my recruiting class at Duke. Moreover, our team included several McDonald's All Americans, as well as lots of guys who were all-state and had realistic dreams of playing professionally. Coach K said to us, "I'm not going to decide who plays and who doesn't; *you* are going to decide. You will determine, with your preparation and your focus and how you play, the opportunities you get in practice and in games. The question is, Do you make our team better?"

So that was the criterion: not who had the best shot, not who scored the most points, but who made the *team* better. I heard this message and I was determined: I was *never* going to be the guy who didn't get to play. I was just never going to be that guy.

Interestingly, our individual roles were never defined for us. It was up to the players themselves to define those roles. And everyone sort of fell in line. It wasn't easy. It was very high pressure. But we had championship aspirations. And when you have championship aspirations, you don't worry about labels; you worry about doing your job well.

Basketball at Duke was a little different from most college programs—it was based on unselfishness. If you were selfish, that would be revealed in film sessions and the subsequent benchings. We watched a ton of film every day. That was how we got the feedback we needed to see where we had room for improvement. The eye in the sky never lies. So, in watching those films, we got direct feedback about our own level of effort and mental focus. If you wanted to play, you had to be able to *think the game*—that is, be mentally present throughout every practice and game. You had to be able to think the game not just sometimes but through every second of every possession.

What makes Coach K better than any other coach in the entire world, in any sport, is his ability to understand every member of his team and what makes each of them tick. It's his ability to unite and inspire the whole group, by connecting with and inspiring each of us in his own special way. That's an unbelievable skill. I have no doubt that if Coach K weren't the world's greatest basketball coach, he'd be running a Fortune 500 company, or he'd be a senator, a great general, or pretty much anything he wanted to be. He just has an uncanny ability to *reach* the people in his circle. In terms of the Coaching Up Model, he's a genius at building authentic connections.

One of the ways he built those connections with each of us was through honest communication. He had a rule: "we communicate with eye contact. When you have something to say, you look me in the eye and say it." That made it real.

For my part, I've never responded well to anyone yelling at me or challenging my manhood, my toughness. I know I'm tough. I know I have heart. So, if you challenged me that way, I would say, "You know what? You're an idiot. You don't know what you're talking about."

Coach K realized this about me. The way he got me to go to another level as a player was to challenge me intellectually. He would challenge my mental capacity to handle the load that it takes to be a top player.

And that drove me crazy. So I was out to prove to him that I was the smartest, most diligent, most focused, and just mentally toughest player he had ever coached. That's what I tried to do every single day.

And he challenged me, he pushed my buttons—in a way that I knew was about love. It was absolutely about love. Though it wasn't always easy.

The story he still tells every time I'm around is this: when I was a junior, I was the team captain. Usually, after the team stretching commenced, the coach would address us all with the key messages of the day: okay guys, we need to get together. We need to really work our man-to-man defense; we need to focus on finishing. We haven't really been sharp the last few days. Whatever the key message of the day was. But for me, as the team captain, and being the mother hen that I was, Duke basketball was *my* program. And so one day I took the initiative to jump in and address the team myself. I said, "Okay guys, this is what we need to do today. This is how we get better." And I went down the line and spelled out how we would get better. Coach K was pretty impressed and said, "What Shane said was better than anything I could have said."

So that became my task, every day: I addressed the team. He let me have ultimate control over my team. I didn't recognize at the time how unusual this arrangement was; for me, leading this team was just what I was supposed to do. But I came to recognize that it takes a really special coach to understand that sometimes it's best to let go. Sometimes, you can achieve the best outcome for your team by allowing your players to take ownership, while you yourself coach less, at least verbally. And the storybook ending we had my senior year was like a movie: winning the last game of the season, having a Final Four run, and then winning the national championship.

The relationship Coach K and I have, it's hard to put into words. It's much deeper than I can explain. There's trust; there's love. I thought I was an extension of him, and I'm sure he thought I was an extension of him, too.

My greatest attributes as a player were my ability to focus and my ability to think the game. That was my job. I would just know, innately, where I needed to be on the court and where my teammates needed to be.

Of course, I wasn't infallible; everybody makes mistakes. But I was lucky; I was pretty autonomous. I didn't need Coach K to tell me when I messed up. I knew when I messed up. Whenever I messed up, I would raise my hand and say, "My bad; it's not going to happen again." And I'd never make that same mistake again. So he didn't generally need to point out my mistakes, because he knew I was aware of them and would correct them.

But every player is different, and he coached each of us according to what we needed. There were some players who needed—let's say—a vigilant, constant reminder of their responsibilities, also known as a kick in the pants; I wasn't one of them.

The deal was, you'd best do what you were supposed to do, or you were going to hear from Coach K. But, again, however he corrected a player, it was never personal. It was about the health and vitality of the team. That focus was always paramount, and everybody knew it. That's what makes *coachability*: the understanding that the health and vitality of the team depend on everybody playing his role. That understanding is the ultimate environment to improve in, both as a player and as a team. Because if you're focused on anything else—if you're not focused on the team—you're not doing your job.

Accepting a Life-Changing Direction

In terms of the Coaching Up Model, Big Ed and Coach K embodied, for me, the extraordinary value of building an authentic connection with a player. They also exemplified, with my high school coaches, the power of providing genuine support. But the coach who best represented for me the transformative potential of offering concise direction was Chip England.

Chip England, who's now the shooting coach with the San Antonio Spurs, is probably the single person most responsible for helping me have the career I've had. I met him at a basketball camp at Duke the summer after my freshman year—he was a Duke alumnus and had played under Coach K his senior year. Chip watched me play awhile and took me aside and said, "Look, if you want to be the pro that I think you want to be, you're going to have to reconstruct your jump shot."

At the time my shot was good enough—it had gotten me to the top of the game in high school, and it had gotten me to Duke—but it wasn't technically efficient.

And I knew it. I had a shot that came up the side slot, instead of the middle slot. This had implications for coming off curls and down screens and pick and rolls. It made the difference between getting the shot off and getting the shot blocked. Any screen that I came off to my left, I would bring the ball back across my body and shoot from my right. Essentially, that side slot shot eliminated half the court as territory from which I could ever make a shot; plus my form was costing me a valuable extra second that you just don't have in the NBA.

Chip England was the most unconventional basketball mind I've ever been around. And by *unconventional*, I mean *brilliant*. I was so lucky to hook up with him. He said, "If you want to be a 10-year NBA veteran, you're going to have to relearn how to shoot the basketball." He intellectualized the game for me by explaining exactly why I needed improvement. And I said, "I'm in. I'm interested. You got me. What do I need to do? I'm all ears."

So, talk about going back to basics. In the middle of an incredibly high-pressure scenario—we were in line to be number one in the country, favorites to win the national championship—there I was, probably the starting power forward, reteaching myself how to shoot.

What made it possible for me to undertake that transformation, in that high-pressure situation, with so much at stake? First, there was a lot of trust. Coach K trusted Chip England because he knew him and had coached him when he played for Duke. And I trusted both Coach K and Chip England. But of course it was still a dicey proposition. As a player, you have to have a level of self-awareness and the ability to understand your own strengths and weaknesses. This can be really hard, especially if you have high aspirations. It's tough to look at yourself honestly and say, "You know what? This isn't working. This isn't good enough. I need to reinvent myself."

So, I deconstructed my shot and built it back up. That was a long, slow, agonizing six- or seven-month process. I didn't shoot well the first half of the year. And then it clicked. January 26, 1999, we played the University of Maryland Terrapins at home. They were major rivals of ours, ranked among the top teams in the country, and had been undefeated that season in the Atlantic Coast Conference (ACC) games on their home court. So it was a huge game. I had been averaging 10 points a game, and that day I scored 27 points, shooting 10/13 from the field and 4/4 on three-pointers. We handed the Terrapins their first and only ACC defeat on their home court that whole season, 82 to 64. And everyone was like, "Who the hell is this Battier kid? Where did this guy come from?"

That seminal game was literally the springboard, the inflection point of my career. That was where everything I'd talked about with Chip and all the work I'd done all came together and gave me the confidence that my new shot was working. For the rest of that season, I averaged something like 15 points a game. The next year it was 20 points, and my senior year it was 21 points. That year I was an all-American, was named national player of the year and national defensive player of the year, and was a first-round draft pick in the NBA. And it all sprang from that one game. It changed my life, literally. One game—after one piece of concise direction and a whole lot of very hard work.

On Playing on a Winning Team

Part of the reason I love this Coaching Up concept and this book is that it resonates so closely with my experience of working with so many great coaches. I've been lucky enough to play for brilliant coaches all up and down the line, and I've learned so much from their different styles and systems.

Big Ed Battier was the first of them, of course. But there were many others: Kurt Keener's won 10 state titles; Coach K's won five national championships; and Hubie Brown is one of the smartest minds in basketball, ever. Jeff Van Gundy is a tremendous, tremendous coach. Rick Adelman is going to be in the Hall of Fame. And Erik Spoelstra just won back-to-back NBA championships.

They have all, each in his own way, practiced the three fundamental elements of the Coaching Up Model:

building an authentic connection, providing genuine support, and offering concise direction. Some have excelled more in one of those activities, some in others. But they have had all three elements in their coaching repertoires.

Another thing has been consistent across all the great coaches I've played for: their mantra has always been team over self. It's all about the health and vitality of the team. If you're not willing to help the whole team go in a positive direction, then you're not only doing a disservice to the team but also doing a huge disservice to yourself. When you give yourself fully to the team and to the journey—body, mind, and soul—that's when you reach your full potential as a player, and that's when your team reaches its full potential as a group.

The great Hubie Brown used to tell us, "Listen, when you retire, nobody's ever going to ask you how many points did you average, how many rebounds, how many steals. They'll ask you one question: 'did you win?'"

From my own experience as a two-time NBA champion, that question often takes the form "Where do you keep your rings?" or "How do you choose which ring you're going to wear?" Aren't those awesome questions? And aren't those the ones you want to be answering?

Kids get caught up in their statistics. They need to be told, "Don't worry about that." If you're a good player—a real player, a team player—recruiters will find you. You will not fall through the cracks. Do you understand the amount of money spent on scouting and finding good players?

If you're a player, just keep this in mind: it's much easier to be found, and to distinguish yourself, when you're part of a winning team. If you're on a losing team and you put up great numbers, recruiters will always question your ability to play on a winning team—which is what every coach wants. So focus on helping your whole team be winners.

And if you're a coach, a leader of any kind of enterprise, a parent, a teacher, a counselor, a doctor or nurse, a family member or friend, a member of any kind of tribe or team or work group or community: look for opportunities to practice the Coaching Up Model set forth in this book. There's a lot of wisdom in it. And it feels great to be on both the receiving end of that model and the coaching end. Most important, it really works. I hope you enjoy reading about it, practicing it, and reaping the results.

—Shane Battier,
NCAA and NBA champion

About Shane Battier

Shane Battier graduated with honors from Detroit Country Day School, having won three state championships, the Michigan Mr. Basketball award, and the Naismith national High School Player of the Year award. Four years later he graduated with honors from Duke University with a degree in religion, having made two Final Four appearances, won a national championship, and earned two all-American awards as well as both the Naismith and the John R. Wooden national Player of the Year awards. In the 2001 NBA draft he was the sixth overall selection, chosen by the Memphis Grizzlies. Subsequently, as a member of the Miami Heat, he played a key role in its back-to-back 2012 and 2013 NBA championships, thus achieving a trifecta of championships at the high school, college, and professional levels. During his 12 years in the NBA, he was a two-time NBA All-Defensive Team member as well as a member of the USA Basketball National Team. Today, as a highly regarded motivational speaker, Shane Battier inspires audience members to new heights by showing them how they too can achieve success, no matter what challenges they are looking to conquer. He and his wife, Heidi, devote considerable energy to the Battier Take Charge Foundation, which they established to provide resources for the development and education of underserved youth and teens. Their goal is to encourage and inspire a new generation of potential leaders through educational opportunities and the cultivation of effective leadership skills. Please check out the foundation at www.takechargefoundation.org.

Introduction

"Coaching, I believe, is not a job; it is a most important calling, a sacred and vital activity where we have been given the fortunate opportunity and privilege to guide and mentor others in a nurturing, selfless, passionate environment, instilling in them the profound sense that they can be something other than ordinary."

—Jerry Lynch, PhD, *Coaching with Heart: Taoist Wisdom to Inspire, Empower, and Lead in Sports & Life*

Why This Book?

There's a ton of theory out there on coaching techniques and even more on leadership. What does this book do that the others don't?

Here's the answer: this book presents a simple three-step model that *actually works* to inspire heightened performance virtually every time you use it. This book will change your life.

I know that's a big claim to make. And I don't make it lightly. I've lived through many years of high-pressure situations—as an athlete who's had many coaches, as a coach who's worked with many athletes, and as the business leader of a fast-paced venture-backed company (CoachUp, Inc.). I've also talked with and observed many of our 18,000+ CoachUp coaches in action as they conduct thousands of training sessions every week across the country. Along the way I've benefited from superb, inspirational coaching—and at times I've agonized, along with my teammates, under frankly awful coaching. I've had the great fortune to encounter terrific leaders and managers and mentors, along with a few not-so-great ones. Each has taught me valuable lessons, for better or worse, and I'm grateful to them all.

But nobody taught me the fundamental model for inspiring excellent performance that I am presenting in this book: the Coaching Up Model. I've distilled it from the best practices of the best coaches, teachers, and

business leaders I've observed. Remarkably, those exceptional individuals, despite working in a wide range of
settings, all tend to use quite similar approaches to the one
I'm offering you here.

You may already be using some aspects of the Coaching Up Model. I've been using it myself for years, at first
loosely and somewhat unconsciously, and then more
carefully and precisely as I came to understand its power.
What transforms it—what really empowers you as a
coach/leader/mentor—is using this approach consciously
and deliberately. In its deepest form, once you've really
taken in the Coaching Up Model and felt its power, it can
expand to comprise the entire arc of an ongoing relationship. Within that arc, when you come to a *crunch time*
(that is, a meeting in which you want to encourage
another person to do something important, and to do
it willingly, wholeheartedly, and very well), you can
distill the whole model into a Coaching Up Conversation
that can take place in a few minutes or even faster. The
key thing to know about it is that it actually *works*—
virtually every time.

So here's my suggestion to you: read this book (it will
take you just a couple of hours), get familiar with this
simple model, and try it out. Keep it in mind the next
time you have a crunch time meeting with someone you
care about. And here's my promise: when you go into a
crunch time meeting ready to consciously use the techniques of the Coaching Up Model, you will be amazed at

the results. In effect, you will be coaching the other person *up*. You will see the result in your player's posture, hear it in his or her voice, and feel it in his or her energy level. Being coached up feels *great*!

And note also how great it feels to be on the coaching end of that conversation. Inspiration is a two-way street. It engages, heartens, and energizes both the person being inspired and the person doing the inspiring. Think back to a time when someone really connected with you, supported you, and offered you inspired advice. Wasn't that a fabulous feeling? Well, I bet it felt the same way to the person who gave you that gift.

In *9 Powerful Practices of Really Great Mentors*, Stephen Kohn and Vincent O'Connell make note of the importance of having "emotional radar" to what both you and the person you are mentoring are feeling in the moment: "whereas the best mentors tend to be smart about the more technical elements and nuances of whatever it is they do for a living, they also must show a different kind of intelligence . . . They must have emotional radar that senses what their protégé is feeling, and what they too are feeling during the guidance process."

So, try it out, and see what happens. And let me know what you think, okay? I'm always eager to hear from people who are doing this kind of coaching. And as you go about doing it, keep in mind what John Zenger and Kathleen Stinnett put forth in their book, *The Extraordinary Coach*: "we hope you remember that sometimes, just being willing to engage in the coaching conversation is the best gift that you can offer those around you. Sometimes the medium is the message."

And here's another promise: keep using the Coaching Up Model, and it will very quickly become second nature, like breathing. Moreover, using the model will become even simpler than the already-simple model suggests. That's because when you have Coaching Up Conversations with people you know well, you won't always need to use all three elements of the model. In fact, in some situations, you may be able to conduct an entire Coaching Up Conversation without using any words at all.

Who Can Use the Coaching Up Model?

You don't have to be a sports coach or a business leader to benefit from this model. When you think about it, we're all private coaches at least some of the time. Every day, most of us have dozens of opportunities to encourage, guide, or inspire our fellow human beings. Maybe a colleague at your office has been procrastinating on tackling a tough project. Maybe a family member is nervous about a challenging situation at work or at school. Perhaps a friend is struggling with a major life change. Once you learn the Coaching Up Model, you will find it natural—and amazingly effective—in all these situations.

But let's be real; for quite a few of us, there's nothing like the adrenaline-pumping pressure of intense athletic competition. Finding yourself in a 30-second timeout on a basketball court, when the other team has the ball and is up by one point and there's only a minute left in the game and you have to figure out what to do *fast* has a wonderful way of focusing the mind.

This book is about how to have the kind of *fast, concentrated,* and *highly effective* conversation the coach has with the players on his or her team in that situation—the core communication of which is done via one-on-one conversations. Here you will find a technique that will help you actually get stuff done when the stakes are high. You will discover how to motivate somebody to perform brilliantly.

You will also find this book liberally sprinkled with examples, anecdotes, and observations contributed by coaches and athletes. Many of these are derived from an informal survey we conducted in December 2015 among 200 of the top coaches on CoachUp. Others have come via my observation, reading and research, or by word of mouth.

A few caveats before we get into the model itself.

Despite the effectiveness of this approach, the Coaching Up Model won't work unless you actually care about the person you're working with. (For the purposes of this book, let's continue to use sports as our primary metaphor and call the person doing the coaching the *coach* and the person being coached the *player*.) To be effective as the coach in a Coaching Up Conversation, you don't have to love your player. But you do have to respect your player and care about his or her well-being. And you must really want your player to perform brilliantly *for his or her own sake*, not just for your purposes or the purposes of a larger group. Of course, your player's heightened performance will likely radiate benefits across his or her team, family, and other communities. But you are conducting your Coaching Up Conversation for the player's benefit, full stop.

There are plenty of reasons that any of us can sometimes lose sight of the vital importance of the people we work with. We are all under enormous pressure to do as much as possible as fast as possible, often with limited resources. It's all too easy to find our heads turned and our focus shifted to short-term outcomes, such as winning or profits or productivity. And it's all too easy to fall back on adhering to rigid methodologies or systems, rather than staying in the moment and engaging with the issues and needs of the people right in front of us. The beauty of the Coaching Up Model is that by helping us simply focus on our actual, living relationships, it prevents us from falling into automatic, detached, or remote ways of engaging with others.

One of the key attributes involved in applying the Coaching Up Model, whether in sports or at work or in our personal relationships, is empathy. You must hold yourself open to feeling, clearly and fully, both your own feelings and those of the person you are coaching.

So in practicing the model, please keep in mind three guidelines:

1. Your player must *trust* that you respect him or her and care about his or her well-being and success. As Susan Weinschenk points out in *How to Get People to Do Stuff*, "To get people to trust you, first show them that you trust them. When they trust you, they will be more likely to do what you are asking them to do."

2. And remember that it's not enough for you to respect and care about your player in your private heart of hearts; you've got to communicate it. If your player is someone you work with or live with or see often, then you will have many opportunities to communicate that respect day after day, consistently, in the course of everyday interactions. (I'll say more about how to go about this later.) Building that kind of respectful and trusting relationship is like socking savings away in a bank, but more fun. Joe Ehrmann puts it well in his important book, *InSideOut Coaching*: "players will do what they are told by a Wizard of Oz–type coach, but they will only truly follow someone whom they believe in and who believes in them. Coaching is all about relationships . . . transformational coaching only occurs when people believe in you and choose to follow because they know that you believe in them, too."

3. In conducting a Coaching Up Conversation, you must be both sincere and humble. While it's important to bring your whole best self to this conversation, you must also, paradoxically, take yourself out of it. This is not about you; it's about your player. I'll say more about this, too. As Steve Chandler and Scott Richardson say in *100 Ways to Motivate Others*, "Motivation requires a calm, centered leader, focused on one thing, and only one thing." In these conversations, your focus needs to be on your player.

In the next few chapters I'll first explain how the Coaching Up Model works and then delve into the three basic elements within it. I'll also have some suggestions to offer about how to build the kind of relationships that make Coaching Up Conversations particularly fluid and natural—and so effective that it's even possible to conduct them, under some circumstances, without saying a single word. And then we'll focus on making the model work at work and the special challenges and rewards of using it at home. But we'll get to all that later.

First, let's take a look at the Coaching Up Model.

1

How the Coaching Up Model Works

"Whether the manager likes it or not, creating great relation-ships is how careers are built, how businesses are built, and how great teams are built."
—Steve Chandler and Scott Richardson,
*100 Ways to Motivate Others: How Great
Leaders Can Produce Insane Results
Without Driving People Crazy*

The world is awash in clutter. Our brains are being shaped by the media. Attention spans are shrinking. Videos are getting shorter. Nobody wants to read a long e-mail message, let alone write one. Fewer and fewer people even communicate in whole sentences. (Noticed that? Right!) There's a lot of noise out there. How do you cut through the noise to deliver a critically important message—fast? How do you reach somebody with a transformative, inspiring message in a crunch?

The answer—based on my broad and deep experience as a basketball player who has had many coaches at the high school, collegiate, and professional levels, and as a coach who has coached teams and worked one-on-one and in small groups with basketball players for over a decade—is the very simple process I am calling the Coaching Up Model. Sometimes that model encompasses the full span of an ongoing relationship; at other times, it takes the form of a compact conversation. Here's an example of the conversation.

An Actual Coaching Up Conversation

Let's imagine that you are the trainer/coach for a young heavyweight boxer, who, after just a few months of training, has signed up for his first real match. The match begins. At the end of the first round your boxer emerges from a slugfest in which neither he nor his opponent has gained the upper hand. He returns to his corner for a 1-minute rest before heading out for the second round. He's winded, his legs are tired, the crowd is hostile, his left wrist is throbbing, and he isn't sure whether he will survive the next round. You have 1 minute to communicate with him—what do you do?

The clock is ticking. Your fighter sits down; the assistant trainer slips a towel around his neck. The fighter takes a sip of water, kicks out his legs, and relaxes his arms at his sides, as you've taught him to do for maximum rest. The assistant trainer is applying Vaseline to his face to cover the cuts and prevent future abrasions. Fifty-five seconds. Fifty seconds. You hover over him. He looks up to you for answers. You know your fighter's thoughts: "tell me what to do (quick!). Tell me how to win this thing—or help me get me out of here!" You've got to say something! What do you say?

Well, the boxer in this scenario was actually me. I had been training with a CoachUp boxing coach, Tommy Duquette, a former U.S. Olympic team finalist, to prepare for the one and only heavyweight USA Boxing–sanctioned match in which I would ever participate. It was part of a long evening of matches put on at Boston's House of Blues by Haymakers for Hope—an organization that raises money for cancer research by matching up amateur fighters, whose friends and family members donate money and come to watch the fights.

I don't like fighting. But having lost a grandfather to cancer, as well as several other members of my extended family, I wholeheartedly wanted to support this cause. Besides, I love any opportunity to get close with top coaches and learn from them.

So, to prepare for the fight, I put my trust in Coach Tommy. He is not only one of CoachUp's top boxing trainers but also one of the best, most naturally expert practitioners I have ever known of what I would later come to understand as the heart of the Coaching Up Model.

My opponent and I were about the same size, but his conditioning was superior to mine—he had been training far longer and harder, and belonged to a famous boxing gym. I, on the other hand, rarely trained, had not gone for a run in months (thanks to Achilles tendonitis), and did not belong to a boxing gym. But I had one, and only one, major advantage: I had great private coaching.

In this 1-minute break after the first round, Tommy went to work. There were a million things I'd done wrong in that first round. Moreover, he could tell I was totally gassed. In sparring against the same opponent for practice just four weeks earlier, I had lost in two rounds— and sprained my left wrist in the process. Tommy had considered pulling me from the official match, but I was committed to going through with it. Sitting on the stool and looking up at Tommy, I felt my wrist throbbing. I didn't think I could hit hard with it. Tommy hovered above me, studying me benevolently. The assistant trainer kept applying Vaseline. Forty-five seconds dwindled to 40.

Finally, rather than critiquing my first-round performance (or lack of same), Tommy asked me a question: "J, that has to be your dad in the first row over there, right? I love that he's wearing a suit to this thing. You got to introduce us afterward, yeah? Look how proud he is of you! Has he ever been to a boxing match before?"

Thirty-five seconds remaining, and I said, "I see him. Happy to intro you guys afterward. He definitely hasn't been to a match before, nor does he know anything about boxing. What does this have to do with anything anyway? Tommy, I can't feel my left hand."

Twenty-five seconds left. Tommy leaned in. "Don't worry about that, you did a great job jabbing with it and just keeping him honest. Plus he's scared of your right uppercut. Even though you didn't connect with it, I know he's thinking about it. You totally crushed that round, he's all mentally messed up right now."

Eighteen seconds remaining. "Yeah?" I said, encouraged. "You got any advice for this round?"

Ten seconds remaining. "No, man, you know what you're doing. Oh, when you go out there, give him that 'down up' we worked on . . . You know, bend your knees and give that left jab to the body. Don't worry about connecting. Then do it again right away. Bend your knees and fake the left jab to the body just like before, but shoot that right hand to his chin. He'll drop his hands to protect the body and won't see it coming. Let's go. You got this, bro!"

Two seconds. I stood up, stepped back into the fight, gave my opponent the "down up," and landed my right hand with force, knocking him back across the ring. I won by a technical knockout in the second round, in what turned out to be the single most dominating fight of the evening.

What did Coach Tommy do that made all the difference? He made a *connection* with me as a person, not a function, while temporarily distracting me from the high-pressure situation; provided *support* for my flagging self-esteem after my performance in the first round; and offered me one simple pointer—a concise, concrete *direction* that I could easily follow.

That's the Coaching Up Model:

- Build an authentic *connection*.
- Provide genuine *support*.
- Offer concise *direction*.

It's that simple. Tommy *connected* with me not just as a function—a pitiable fledgling boxer experiencing heavy distress—but as a whole real person, a person who had a dad and indeed an entire actual life that would almost certainly extend into the future after this fight.

Strange though it may seem, an athlete—or anybody, really—can lose sight of solid facts like those in a moment of intense stress. When Tommy had me look at my father, even if only for seconds, it gave me a mental break from thinking about the next round, which, of course, helped me relax. It's incredibly helpful to be lifted out of your current self-focus and into a larger, more heartening reality.

Second, Tommy put a positive spin on that first round that I had been feeling so bad about. He *supported* me by pointing out aspects of my performance—and my opponent's responses—that I was too short-term focused to be able to observe. His observations restored my self-confidence and my sense of at least cautious optimism.

Because Tommy had both connected with me and supported me, I was able to take a deep breath and be sufficiently relaxed, confident, and open to listen eagerly to his *direction*. And because he gave me that direction concisely and at the last possible moment, it stayed fresh in my mind and active in my short-term memory. I didn't have time to second-guess or overthink it. I just acted, and my training took over and made my action effective.

Time spent on each component of this minute-long Coaching Up Conversation:

- Building an authentic *connection*: 35 seconds
- Providing genuine *support*: 15 seconds
- Offering concise *direction*: 10 seconds

And that's important to note. As a coach, you need to make the largest investment in building an authentic connection. Without that, the genuine support you provide won't seem so genuine, and your player may very well second-guess your direction.

Over time, as you invest again and again in building that connection and providing support, you not only earn the ability to offer direction—much of which is at the request of your player, now that trust has been formed—but also position yourself to communicate effectively in time-sensitive conversations.

If you've ever been fortunate enough to have a player, employee, or friend say to you something along the lines of "Don't sugarcoat the truth. I know you have my best interests in mind, so just give it to me straight—what should I do about XYZ?" you know that you have built an authentic connection with that person. You don't need to spend the first 30 minutes of an hour-long one-on-one conversation reinforcing the connection, then supporting the person, before you can get into the meat of the topic and your actual thoughts about what course of action should be taken. You can skip over steps 1 and 2 and jump right into the direction. Furthermore, you can make that direction concise. What's concise direction? Here are two ways of saying the same thing, concisely and verbosely:

Concise Direction: "Oh, when you go out there, give him that 'down up' we worked on."

Verbose Direction: "I think it would be really good if you could land a big punch at the start of this match. I noticed that you haven't thrown anything to his body, so if you start out by throwing a body shot, he will think it's for real and will drop his left arm to cover the ribs. Then, probably, after he blocks your first punch, you can throw the same exact left to the body again, which will cause him to think because you are an amateur boxer you are trying the same thing again, and he will drop his left arm again to block it. So, if you fake that second punch, and instead bring it back and shoot a right hand over the top of his left hand, you may catch his chin. He probably won't tuck his chin, because he isn't very experienced either, and if you can catch him with a strong right at the start of the match, you can get the upper hand and jump all over him and maybe earn a few points that will carry the round for you. On the other hand, if he doesn't go for your fake, you will be exposed to his right hand over the top and he may hurt you with it. But I still think it's probably a risk we should take to start the round. Okay, cool. Let's do this . . ."

Why didn't Tommy have to explain that whole thing to me? Why was he able to keep his direction concise, and why was I so able to take it in and follow it? It's simple.

First, I trust Tommy. I trust him because we have an authentic connection and he genuinely supports me—not just as a boxer but as a person who has a life, a family ("Look at your dad in the front row!"), and multiple interests outside the ring. So when Tommy says to do something, I'm going to do it.

Second, it was the last thing Tommy said to me as I stood up to enter the next round, so it was fresh in my mind.

Third, it was superconcise; there was no way I could forget his direction.

Fourth, I knew what he meant by the "down up" fake, because he had taught it to me and I had practiced it hundreds of times.

And fifth, I *knew* it would work in this situation. I knew it because I knew that Tommy knew me—my strengths, my weaknesses, my mental state—and that he also knew those aspects of my opponent. Tommy was literally in that ring with me. For instance, he knew that my left hand was killing me, so all I could do was fake with it. And he knew that my legs were tired, so if I didn't do that "down up" fake to start the round, I probably wouldn't have the strength to do it at the end of the round. Tommy's vast knowledge of boxing enables him to be a great fighter; his ability to communicate through the Coaching Up Model enables him to be a great coach.

In Contrast, the Showboat Approach

The above anecdote is a prime example of a Coaching Up Conversation. We may find it instructive to take a look at its polar opposite approach—what we might think of as the Coaching Down or Showboat approach. This is the coaching model we've all seen and heard far too often on school playgrounds and in gyms and even on professional playing fields everywhere. Whether during a 60-second timeout in basketball or a 60-second break between rounds in a boxing match, a Showboat coach will jump right into the lesson—pouring forth as much criticism, advice, observation, and information as possible into a short period.

A Showboat coach believes that good coaching involves:

1. Actively packing verbal communication into every available second
2. Providing as much criticism and as many orders as possible before the referees call the players back into the game, before the bell rings, or until the players' water break is over
3. Trying to pump players up by shouting, arm waving, fist pumping, and so on

How does a Showboat coach criticize a player? As frequently, loudly, and passionately as possible. He or she pulls the player aside, yells into the player's face, and waves his or her arms, broadcasting extreme dissatisfaction with the previous play or the player's overall performance. The coach makes sure that not only the player but also the rest of the team, and even the player's friends, family members, and other fans in the stands, can feel the humiliation.

This coach appears to be "really coaching"—often sweating, red in the face, clapping his or her hands aggressively, and using dominating/authoritative gestures. If you were to draw a cartoon or choose a stock online image of a coach, you would very likely base it on a Showboat coach. And that's exactly the point. How unfortunate that this conception of coaching is so prevalent in our society. The fact that this image leaps to mind as familiar demonstrates the extent of the problem. Many coaches fail to heed Sam Walton's simple yet profound advice from his decades of experience founding and running Wal-Mart: "outstanding leaders go out of their way to boost the self-esteem of their personnel. If people believe in themselves, it's amazing what they can accomplish."

Before we come down too hard on the Showboat coach, let us freely admit that all of us—myself certainly included—have been there to some extent at one time or another. It's easy, in the heat of battle, given the pressures and challenges that coaches, business leaders, and parents face with time constraints, overwhelming demands, and limited resources, to focus on going for quick results. It's only natural that we tend to fall back on the old models of coaching that we've all been exposed to. Even the most masterful and apparently natural practitioners of the Coaching Up Model will likely admit that it took

them years to get to where they are. It takes time to shed
bad habits and learn the key principles of great coaching:
that it's never about the coach but about the relationship,
and that when it comes to communicating effectively, less
is more.

From the perspective of Showboat coaches, any
coaches who are not broadcasting their thoughts as
frequently, passionately, and vigorously as possible just
aren't doing their job. After all, in every play, attentive
coaches notice so many mistakes and flaws that it's their
duty to point them all out and make sure the players
correct them, right?

Oh so wrong. The Showboat coaches are in fact
undercutting their own effectiveness.

If you stopped a Showboat coach in the moment and
asked, "What do you hope to achieve by criticizing your
player so passionately?" the coach would likely respond
that "This is tough love" or "This is the only way to get
through to my players, so that they can learn from their
mistakes" or "Gosh darn it, I've told him a thousand times
not to do it that way, and he just won't listen, so I have to
try something else."

But the underlying truth—which the Showboat
coach is *not* saying here — is that the player's bad play
or performance reflects poorly on the coach. The Showboat coach's real motivation is not to improve the player's
performance, but to make it clear to everyone—the
player, the team, the fans, and whoever else may be

watching and blaming the coach—that "it's not my fault. The athlete just won't listen to me and is not doing what I told him or her to do."

Most important, how would you feel if you were the athlete in this situation?

If you've ever played Little League baseball, Pop Warner football, or any other youth or high school sport, you've probably witnessed coaching like this. Maybe you've even felt the brunt of it. I've been there, and it's a horrible feeling. You're already feeling bad enough about making a mistake. Now you've been pulled from the game and humiliated in front of your teammates, the opposition, maybe even scouts and the press, and likely both friends and family members in the stands. You were already angry with yourself, and you're still feeling that way. But now, in addition, you're even angrier with your coach.

Fortunately, people are becoming more aware of the negative effects this type of coaching has on young athletes. Entire organizations, such as the Positive Coaching Alliance, have formed to preach an alternative, more positive style to coaches, parents, and athletes around the country. As Joe Ehrmann notes in *InSideOut Coaching*, "I have seen the good, the bad, and the ugly faces of the coaching vocation. I am certain of one thing: coaches can either break young people's psyches or build their souls."

But I've found that the problem is not limited to athletic playing fields at the youth, collegiate, and even professional levels. In fact, most businesses—from start-ups to Fortune 500 companies—suffer from "managers" who practice the Showboat coaching style. They quite literally coach down their employees in a variety of contexts—both in one-on-one weekly sessions and in public in front of other colleagues. In behaving this way, Showboat coach/managers broadcast their position of authority, highlight their vast knowledge and experience, and express anger or disappointment in work that is less than what they could have produced or expect any competent person to produce.

When you find yourself at the receiving end of direction from a Showboat coach, what happens to you? Very likely, you are no better positioned to avoid the mistake you just made or to get back into the game mentally. Instead, your coach has done a disservice to you, and to your entire team, from his or her self-interested goal of wanting to heap blame onto your shoulders. You've ended up demoralized and dejected. The coach has coached you *down*, not *up*.

Showboat coaches—and Showboat managers and Showboat parents—are not necessarily bad people. They're just misguided. They don't understand the underlying truth behind all communication: force-feeding doesn't nourish; shouting doesn't communicate; humiliation doesn't inspire.

The fundamental distinction between the Showboat approach to coaching and the Coaching Up approach is that *the Showboat approach is all about the coach, and the Coaching Up approach is all about the player.* Unfortunately, the problem is widespread not only in sports but also in the corporate world.

The Rewards of Coaching Up Conversations

By learning to engage the people we care about in Coaching Up Conversations, we can all become better communicators with our colleagues, parents, partners, children, and friends. Through understanding the underlying reasons why this model works, and then coming up with our own authentic ways of using it, we can get really good at motivating others to achieve breakthrough performance. Plus, engaging in this kind of conversation feels terrific.

One of the common objections I frequently hear from overworked and overstressed executives and coaches is that "I simply don't have the time for building relationships—I need to get fast results!" On the basis of my experience using the Coaching Up Model as an athlete, a coach, and a business leader at CoachUp, I believe that this objection is shortsighted. *The Coaching Up Model is an investment in an instrument that allows you to communicate with maximum efficiency, at those times when it matters most.* Precisely because you have built an authentic relationship, you are able to communicate efficiently and effectively at those critical moments when it counts most, whether the game is on the line or your organization is at an inflection point. To those coaches and executives who say, "I don't have the time to invest in this kind of relationship building," I respond, how can you afford not to? It's an investment in your ultimate success that pays countless dividends.

So now let's explore, one by one, the three basic elements of a Coaching Up Conversation and the broader Coaching Up Model: *building an authentic connection, providing genuine support,* and *offering concise direction.*

2

Building an Authentic Connection

"Whereas the best mentors tend to be smart about the more technical elements and nuances of whatever it is they do for a living, they also must show a different kind of intelligence . . . They must have emotional radar that senses what their protégé is feeling, and what they too are feeling during the guidance process."
—Stephen E. Kohn and Vincent D. O'Connell,
9 Powerful Practices of Really Great Mentors: How to Inspire and Motivate Anyone

So, what's an authentic connection between two human beings? In my view, it's one in which both people feel truly seen, known, and respected. Such connections can grow organically through long acquaintance, for instance between family members, longtime friends, or colleagues who have worked together for years. Or they can be established quite quickly by people who have the skill, desire, and grace, to put energy into doing it. Barack and Michelle Obama, for instance, both excel at connecting almost instantly with people they talk with. Can you think of other leaders who have that apparently innate gift of charisma? Other politicians who are master communicators, such as John Kennedy, Ronald Reagan, and Bill Clinton, come to mind, along with revered athletes such as Stephen Curry, Tom Brady, Magic Johnson, and David Ortiz, and media personalities such as Oprah Winfrey.

You recognize the people who have this ability. Whether you are a Republican or a Democrat, a fan of the Lakers or the Celtics, you can tell that some politicians have it and some athletes have it, while others just don't. They may be really smart, they may have great ideas, they may be very talented, but they aren't able to quickly win people's trust. For instance, having grown up in Boston, and obviously being a lifelong Celtics fan, I may not like the Lakers very much, but I cannot deny the brilliance of Magic Johnson, not only as a player and a man, but also as a charismatic leader. He's someone you instantly feel you know or would love to know. Magic gets it. People like Magic can both form authentic connections with other people and inspire people to want to follow them. Were they just born with this gift? No. It's a thing that can be studied and learned. How do people who have this power achieve it?

For one thing, they focus not on themselves but on the person they are speaking to. This takes some getting used to. When it comes to communicating, most of us naturally focus on ourselves as speakers. We slip into our Speaking Mode, absorbed in questions such as: what should I say? How should I say it? How well am I coming across? The last place we are is exactly where we should be—fully present in the moment with the person or people we're talking with. From the point of view of effective communication, we may be working very hard, but we are not working very smart. We are operating in the dark, making random guesses as to what may really be on the other person's mind, without any targeting whatsoever. To make matters worse, being in our own heads as we are, we are far more likely to miss whatever clues a person is actually sending us.

When we switch to the Listening Mode, everything changes. Now all our effort in communication goes into understanding where the other person is, what might be most helpful to him or her at that moment, and the terms in which he or she can best be reached. Now, when we finally decide to speak, we are more effective because whatever we say will be directed, concise, and to the point. Instead of operating in the dark, making random points that are of no interest to our listener, we are now working at maximum efficiency. Whatever carefully considered comments we choose to make have a far greater chance of hitting their mark and being heard.

The essence of effective coaching is great communication, and the core of great communication is not great speaking but great listening. The good news here is that it is so much easier to be a great listener than it is to be a great speaker. Listening Mode requires only making a commitment to developing the habits and basic skills of a listener. Many people do not think they can be successful communicators because they are not articulate speakers or because they may tend toward the shy, quiet, or introverted end of the spectrum. But when you communicate primarily through Listening Mode, these exact qualities that seem at odds with success for someone in Speaking Mode are your very strengths.

Anyone can be a great listener by simply determining to be one and by practicing a few basic active-listening skills. First seek to ask open-ended questions that don't lead to abrupt, closed yes-or-no answers. Toward this end take advantage of the five *w*s + *h*: *who, what, where, when, why,* and *how.* By following up on whatever someone says with simple questions that begin with one of these six words, we avoid overly elaborate and wordy statements and questions (really a disguised reversion to our Speaking

Mode). We also stay focused on the person in front of us and his or her train of thought until we reach the point at which we have something meaningful to say.

With your Listening Mode in place, the key principles that contribute to building an authentic connection in a Coaching Up conversation are actually pretty simple:

- If possible, choose the setting for maximum comfort.
- Greet your player warmly and personally.
- Begin the conversation with a human connection, not a functional one.
- Keep your posture relaxed, and speak slowly, clearly, and thoughtfully.
- Stay focused on your player.
- Practice humor and humility.

If Possible, Choose the Setting for Maximum Comfort

You won't always have a choice about the setting for your Coaching Up Conversation. Sometimes the opportunity for this kind of conversation arises suddenly, and the conversation needs to happen then and there. No matter. Authentic connections are infinitely transportable. But when you have a choice, consider shifting the location for this important conversation away from the day to day setting in which you and your player work or live.

Even under the most seemingly hostile circumstances or conditions, it is always possible with just a word, glance, or gesture to signal to someone your intention to communicate with them in a special and personal way. Often that intention alone, rather than any lengthy content, is sufficient to achieve your end. One of my favorite examples of this occurs in one of the all-time classic sports movies, *Hoosiers*. This movie was based on the true (though heavily fictionalized) story of a boys' high school basketball team from the (fictional) rural Indiana town of Hickory, who overcame tremendous odds to win the 1952 state championship. They did it by playing as a team, led by transformational coach Norman Dale, played by Gene Hackman.

The moment of truth comes in a critical game near the end of their basketball season. The hugely over-achieving Hickory team is trailing by one point with seconds left in the game. Because of a shortage of players, the team is forced to play with its equipment manager and least talented player, Ollie McLellan, who is sent to the free throw line to take two critical free throws, both of which he must make for the team to recover the lead.

The opposing team calls a time-out to "freeze" Ollie. Coach Dale starts addressing his players on the bench about what they are to do after Ollie makes both free throws—what kind of defense they will play and what various scenarios they might encounter in the final seconds of the biggest game of their lives. Ollie is sitting there listening to Coach Dale, a bundle of jittery nerves. This is a kid who hasn't played all year, and suddenly the entire fortunes of not just the team and the school but also the entire town depend on him. Clearly, this situation was not optimized for comfort. But in the middle of this intensely high-pressure situation, addressing his whole team, Coach Dale then says, "After Ollie makes both free throws,"—and turning to Ollie says, "*and you will make them . . .*" and then continues back into his strategy for the ensuing defensive possession.

Coach Dale doesn't lecture Ollie on how to shoot a free throw or try to hypnotize Ollie into believing he can make them. He just gives him a simple message of support at a time when confidence building is the central direction the coach needs to communicate. More important, it's a classic example of finding time, in the middle of a public venue, and in front of the entire team and thousands of fans in the arena, to create a private moment between a coach and a player.

Armed with increased confidence, and the belief of his coach, Ollie heads out of the time-out, confidently sinks both free throws, and becomes a champion, immortalized in the history books as a legend of Indiana basketball.

If you really pause to think about this scenario, you will very likely recognize the value of that one-on-one connection. With just a shift of your attention or energy, you can carve out a special moment of communication with anyone.

Of course, you can also make a larger gesture of connection. Think how it feels when a colleague suggests getting drinks, walking across the street for coffee, or meeting at his or her house for a cookout. Don't you immediately begin to relax? This is about forming a connection. This invitation shows that the person is recognizing you as a human being, not just a colleague, and wants to build a more personal relationship with you. Imagine if you reach out to a colleague and suggest getting together for breakfast, and your colleague responds with "I'm busy. Let's just meet in the office. I'll book a conference room for us." How do you feel? You're probably left thinking something along the lines of "Hmm, I guess I'm just a function for this person, someone who can help him get his work done, and not of much value or use outside that role." How will that perspective affect your conversation in the conference room, when the meeting happens? Will you be in the same state of mind entering the room as you would have been had your colleague responded with "Absolutely! Let's do it. Breakfast at 8:30 on Monday? Looking forward to catching up outside the office for once. It's about time!"

So, how can you do this in practice? Well, if you work together in an office, you could suggest grabbing breakfast or lunch, as in the example above, or simply getting a little air. Just walking together in harmony establishes a kind of connection. Maybe take a stroll to a nearby park or coffee shop for your conversation.

If you're planning a conversation with a friend or family member, think of a setting in which the other person is likely to feel relaxed and comfortable. Sometimes, if the conversation is on a deeply personal topic, you may want to talk in a room with a door that closes, for privacy. At other times, your office, your kitchen table, or a park bench overlooking a stretch of river or pond can feel just right. I generally prefer walking; if you are walking in the same direction with your player, you are instinctively working together—expanding similar energy and already making progress toward a mutual goal of arriving somewhere. You are therefore both in the right environment to have a positive conversation. Plus, being outside—in fresh air and (with luck) sunshine—combined with physical exercise, naturally puts us human beings in a better mood.

Greet Your Player Warmly and Personally

In any one-on-one situation between two people, the most essential principle is to be authentic. At the same time, it's incumbent on the person who holds more power or authority in the relationship to do the work of connecting, inviting the other person into the conversation, welcoming him or her, and making him or her comfortable. In *How to Get People to Do Stuff*, Susan Weinschenk cuts straight to the point: "you'll be more persuasive when you look directly at a person and use a slight smile."

The Verbal Greeting

So when you greet your player, be sure to look directly into his or her eyes and say something like "Great to see you" or "So glad to have this chance to catch up with you." Take this opportunity to reassure your player, right from the first moment, that you value him or her and are glad to be in his or her presence. By all means use casual, comfortable, incomplete sentences; they feel more natural and authentic than a tight-laced "Good morning, X. Thank you for taking the time to meet with me. I am very glad to see you today." I mean, who *talks* like that any more? That sort of stiff formality would be off-putting to pretty much everyone in contemporary U.S. culture.

Here's another suggestion that may feel counter-intuitive: In greeting your player warmly and personally, it's best *not* to call her or him by name. The use of someone's given name establishes a certain distance, even a level of formality. Nicknames are another matter. Nicknames, so long as they are friendly ones that the player enjoys, are badges of inclusion. Why are there always nicknames on teams? The nickname establishes a special relationship. If you know the person's generally used nickname, and it feels natural to use it, go ahead with a "Hey, Bomber, great to see you." And note that little things matter—it's "Hey, Bomber" not "Hi, Bomber," because even "Hi" can be perceived as relatively formal. You start a really formal letter with "Dear Mr./Ms. X," a slightly less formal letter with "Hi John/Mary," a more informal letter with "Hey J/M," and a thoroughly informal note with a "Yo Buddy" or something similar, or just by jumping right into the message. If you want to signal that you respect and recognize the other person as an equal, as a friend, as an insider, take the overt formality out of your greeting.

In fact, I don't think I have a single friend who calls me by my full first name, Jordan. It's "J," "Fliegel," "Fleegs," or any of an infinite number of variations on those themes, based on how well someone knows me. When I hear people say "Jordan," my first thought is that these are people who don't know me very well or with whom I've failed to build an authentic connection. If they knew that I trusted them and valued their friendship, they would likely feel comfortable enough to keep it simple with a "J."

Here's another way to think about this: when you send an e-mail message to a colleague with whom you have a long-standing, positive, and (we hope) authentic relationship, do you sign off with your full name or even your full first name? My experience suggests it's unlikely. I imagine you use an abbreviation, such as your nickname or first initial. Or perhaps you don't include your name at all—after all, he or she knows who you are from your e-mail address, and if you have a real relationship, he or she won't be offended by your not taking the extra seconds to type out your name.

Furthermore, it's really a sign of respect to keep your e-mail short by avoiding the formal greeting and formal conclusion; it sends a clear message that "you and I have an authentic connection so I don't need to observe all these formalities and can get straight to the point, the purpose of my e-mail, my *concise direction.*" As legendary University of California–Los Angeles basketball coach John Wooden once famously said when describing his success in reaching and motivating his players: "It's simple; there's a lot of love in my coaching." Try to demonstrate that quality in every e-mail message you send, precisely by taking out any formality that indicates a lack of true warmth.

The Physical Greeting—or Not

In greeting your player, you may also want to make initial physical contact when and as appropriate. This is a tricky area. Physical contact nowadays is awash in hazards. In our culture, at least, adult men and women must be very careful not to make any physical contact with other adults or youths that could possibly be misinterpreted as overly familiar, intimate, or sexual. On the other hand, it's a natural impulse to reach out and touch someone in greeting, and it's a great way to connect on a person-to-person level. You just have to know the cultural rules.

In France, Belgium, and Italy, for instance, it's completely normal for adults to actively embrace an acquaintance of either gender in greeting, not only with hugs but also with kisses on both cheeks. In fact, in some situations, the failure to embrace in this way would be considered rude. In the United States, however, people may greet friends that way when they meet up outside of work situations but would not normally do so in the office. Here, businesspeople in many professions still habitually employ the formal handshake. There's nothing wrong with a handshake if the culture of your organization endorses that form of greeting. And you can humanize a handshake by accompanying it with a sincere smile and verbal greeting or by placing your other hand over the clasped hands of the handshake to emphasize the warmth of your welcome.

Still, in less formal cultures—the startup community comes to mind, as do sporting events and social events—a handshake can be off-putting. In fact, it can do damage. It signals: "we are not close; I am relating to you formally, not personally." Options for physical contact with acquaintances in those situations may include, depending on your gender, age, and relationship with the other person, hugs, cheek kissing, fist bumping, high fives, pounding each other's shoulders, and so on. Some informal offices (CoachUp's office, for instance) tend to see a lot of fist bumps and high fives. These have the advantage of being informal, casual, peer-to-peer connections. They serve to reinforce warm connections that have already been established. And, perhaps most important, they mimic the behavior used on sports teams, where chemistry and teamwork are often much stronger than in the corporate world.

But remember that your physical greetings, much like your posture, must at all times demonstrate not only warmth and vulnerability but also confidence. "People are more likely to do what you want them to do when they consider you to be a leader. To be seen as a leader, you must show confidence via your body posture and stance," Susan Weinchenk adds.

A Brilliant Casual Greeting

One of the best examples in my experience of a culturally relevant greeting—and a true example of deploying the Coaching Up Model with very few words—came from David Ortiz, the phenomenal baseball slugger known to thousands of adoring Red Sox fans as "Big Papi." I had been trying to meet him for ages, as I wanted to discuss projects that I thought would be mutually interesting, but our schedules never coincided. Then one night I attended the big charity fundraiser in Boston for his Children's Fund—raising money for pediatric services for kids in need in both New England and the Dominican Republic—and there he was. He was with a mutual acquaintance, who signaled me over to introduce us.

The place was packed and jumping, the noise overwhelming, and, of course, the focus was on the important work his charity was doing. Clearly this was no place for an actual conversation. But Ortiz looked me right in the eye, grinned, walked over to me, reached out that powerful right arm to engage me in a dap (the quick, less formal version of a handshake), and said to me: "You good?"

To which I grinned back and said, "I'm great. Awesome event."

And he nodded, and I told him how much I was looking forward to sitting down with him soon, and he said "Likewise." We bumped fists and nodded again, he posed for a photo with my date (which made her night), and that was that. No more than 30 seconds, start to finish.

Why was this so inspiring to me? After all, hadn't he just come over to say hi? Why did it feel like so much more than that?

The answer is that it felt like a complete conversation, as though all the important things had been sorted out, which they had. He signaled that he recognized me in an *authentic connection.* He went out of his way to greet me as a peer, which I am not. He skipped any formalities that would have suggested, "I don't know you, Mr. Random Business Guy" and skipped over the "Hi" and went right to the kind of peer greeting that he would have given to a longtime friend. He then delighted my date by offering a quick pic with her, again *genuinely supporting* me by signaling that he values the new connection. My date may have left thinking, "Wow, David Ortiz actually cares about J for some reason," which, David being the huge star that he is, certainly makes me look good, right? And I came away feeling that we would talk again, under different circumstances, when it made sense. That was David's *concise direction* to me; it could have been translated as "I am obviously busy right now, but I know who you are, and I'm open to considering doing something with you, so I'm going to go out of my way to quickly make you realize that."

That casual, peer-to-peer greeting has stayed with me ever since as a fine model for interactions with others in the startup world, sports world, or other casual settings, not to mention in more traditional corporate settings, where very often a leader can stand out just by acting like a genuine human being. In my view, that kind of greeting should be used in just about every setting in the United States, and in cultures similar to ours, by any leader who wants to build authentic connections. I like to think of it as "The Ortiz."

Let's review what David Ortiz did and how it worked. He is a superstar; I am not. It was his charity's big night. He could have shown superiority in how he greeted me, or in choosing not to greet me. But he chose a very different path that left me inspired and excited about finding ways to work together. David Ortiz has *it*—that charisma thing. The rest of us can learn from what he does and why it works so well. In less than a minute, and by saying only "You good?" and "Likewise," he (1) built an authentic connection with me, (2) gave me genuine support, and (3) offered me concise direction.

Are we reading too much into this? Was he just coming over to say hi? If you asked someone like David Ortiz, or Barack Obama, to break down how they build so many strong relationships and leave everyone they touch inspired and fully in their camps, they would likely not be able to analyze precisely how they do it or to label it as we are doing here. But they definitely have the gift of being able to make it happen. It's like an elite athlete who reacts in an instant when making a dazzling play but can't describe afterward how he or she knew to do it, or a writer banging away at a keyboard typing 100 words a minute, who couldn't tell you where the *W* key is but never has to look for it. There's a lot of muscle memory contributing to a fundamental system that works.

The bottom line: If you are uncertain about employing any of these forms of physical contact in greeting the person you're having a Coaching Up Conversation with, then play it safe and pack the warmth of your welcome into your verbal greeting and facial expression.

Begin the Conversation with a Human Connection, Not a Functional One

Be sure that you don't launch right into the issue at hand. Take the time to check in with your player person to person, not coach to player, leader to employee, or parent to child. Ask open-ended questions (not yes/no questions) that invite him or her to connect with you: "so, how's it going?" "How are things with you?" "How're you doing?" "What's new?" "How was your weekend?"

You are asking these questions because you really want to elevate this conversation above a strictly functional, coach-to-player, leader-to-employee, parent-to-child conversation. This is between two human beings, full stop. It gives you a chance to let the player take the conversation in a direction that will be more intimate—a direction that will strengthen your peer-to-peer relationship, providing an opening for authenticity. On the basis of your player's response to the question, see whether you can either find an opportunity to go deeper into the connection or move on to providing support.

You probably are doing this already, but subconsciously. Ever asked, "How was your weekend?" and the other person says that he or she took the family fishing, or to the beach, or whatever? Very likely you naturally followed up with support along the lines of "Oh, nice. Beautiful weather last weekend, must have been great out there on the lake." Why do you feel a need to say that? Well, because intrinsically, you *want* to connect and support this person. You want him or her to know that you care about, respect, and value him or her as a person. If he or she told you what he or she did over the weekend, and you didn't say anything positive, you could be signaling that you think those weekend plans were questionable, or even worse, that you don't really care and were just asking the question to make small talk—an impression someone might gather if you didn't respond at all to his or her answer.

By the way, the classic office water cooler or coffee station is exactly where conversations around the weekend, the family, or vacation plans come up and where authentic connections are attempted and genuine support is often provided. We all do it. We just don't tend to put much thought into it. The great thing about bringing it to our attention is that we can then act deliberately to form human connections rather than conducting functional conversations.

A key element of maintaining an authentic connection throughout any Coaching Up Conversation is actively noticing how both you and the other person are feeling. Another mental model for this kind of relationship is mentoring. As Stephen E. Kohn and

Vincent D. O'Connell say in their book, *9 Powerful Practices of Really Great Mentors: How to Inspire and Motivate Anyone*, "Effective mentors gauge emotional reactions from protégés to certain stimuli, such as a prodding question or discussion of a prior troublesome event. Mentors need to be comfortable reflecting the feelings of their protégés and owning up to their own while mentoring is underway."

If nothing else, I hope this book helps you recognize when you do act to form authentic connections in your everyday life. I hope it makes you more conscious of the process—including noticing how the other person feels when you practice it and how good it makes you feel, too.

Keep Your Posture Relaxed, and Speak Slowly, Clearly, and Thoughtfully

As your player responds to your greeting, and as the conversation continues, note his or her body language. Is he or she tense, nervous, anxious? Many people feel anxious in one-on-one conversations with people in positions of authority, even if they already know and like the other person. You can help your player relax by deliberately relaxing your own body. A vastly under-appreciated form of human connection is the way we unconsciously pick up cues from other people's body language. By some estimates, 80 percent of communication is nonverbal. So, be aware of what you are communicating nonverbally. Throughout the conversation, keep your posture relaxed. (Of course, you want to be respectful, too; no feet on desks!) It's hard to stay tense in the presence of someone who is relaxed, comfortable, attentive, and pleased to be in the conversation.

And if your player brings up a particularly important or sensitive point, lean in. Get closer. Maybe take off your glasses, if you're wearing them. Use your posture to communicate your sincere interest in what this person is saying to you.

In the same vein, as the conversation proceeds, remember to speak slowly, clearly, and thoughtfully. Relaxed leaders allow space for reflection, rather than rattling off long strings of words. When you listen to experts discussing a topic, they often pause before answering a question, to give it their full consideration. And then they boil down their response to as concise a formulation as possible. Finally, they know when to stop. They don't keep blathering on just to fill the silence. Silence is okay! In *The Extraordinary Coach*, John Zenger and Kathleen Stinnett articulate this final point well by encouraging leaders to practice the acronym W.A.I.T.— "W.A.I.T." as in "Why Am I Talking?" The authors go on to point out that when we are truly trying to understand our coachee's current state of mind, we would do well to keep this handy acronym in mind—and that the person being coached should be talking at least 75 percent of the time.

Stay Focused on Your Player

This is the core of the authentic connection you want to establish (or reinforce, if you've already established it). You want to stay focused on your player both physically and mentally. Remember: this meeting is *not about you.* This meeting is *all about your player.*

The first rule of staying focused on your player is *maintaining eye contact.* This means exactly what it says. Look your player in the eye continuously. Of course, you don't want to take this to silly extremes; you're allowed to blink as needed. You can also occasionally glance away when deep in thought, as you mull over something the other person has asked you, to give it your full, thoughtful attention before responding. But in general, maintain eye contact, full stop.

And when you do speak, feel free to use hand gestures to illustrate your point. As Susan Weinschenk notes, "Using no hand gestures at all conveys a lack of interest. Make sure the people you are talking to can see your hands. If they can't see your hands, it will be hard for them to trust you."

The second rule of staying focused is this: don't do anything else! Above all, *do not multitask.* Don't play

around with your pencil or peek at your cell phone, don't
doodle, and certainly don't read, let alone answer, e-mail
messages. When you multitask, you are damaging your
connection with the other person. Think about the cost
in those terms. It's not just that you might miss or
misconstrue what he or she is saying: there is a real
expense to damaging the connection. You're almost
better off not having the meeting at all.

When I was first launching CoachUp, I was really bad
at this. I was so busy running around putting out fires that
I never felt I had the time just to sit and listen to someone
for half an hour. But unless you give the person you are
talking with your entire, focused attention, you are
actively communicating that you don't value what he
or she is saying. You are claiming that you have priorities
way above your connection with him or her. Moreover,
you are revealing that you are disorganized, that you
don't even know your own priorities, because very likely
you set this meeting. If you've ever made a presentation,
or just raised a point of view, in a meeting in which other
people were on their phones or computers, I'm sure you
will recall how it made you feel. And conversely, if
you've been in the presence of someone who gave
you his or her undivided attention, you will surely
remember how great that felt.

The more you can focus on the person you are talking
with, the more respected he or she will feel. If you know
anyone who is close with Tom Brady, the first thing he or

she will say about Tom is that when you are in his presence, you have the feeling that you have his entire attention. He looks you right in the eye, and he listens. And he's Tom Brady! If there is anyone alive who might feel entitled not to treat regular mortals this way, it's Tom. So the fact that he does look at you, and he does listen, makes *that much stronger an impact.*

And the third rule—possibly the hardest to follow for some of us—is this: *avoid the first-person singular.* If you feel tempted to utter a sentence that begins with *I,* think it over. Does it truly enrich the conversation? Will it be helpful to the person you're with? Or is it purely about you?

This is not a hard-and-fast rule. It's okay to talk about yourself a little from time to time, when it feels directly relevant to the conversation. But in general, in a Coaching Up Conversation, keep your focus on the person you're talking to.

Practice Humor and Humility

These are the two most important qualities you can bring to a Coaching Up Conversation. Although humor and humility are two very different things, they stem from a common core: both are grounded in vulnerability. When a leader shows himself or herself as vulnerable, that leader becomes real. The real leader is someone followers can relate to. He or she provides a green field for authentic connections.

When you try to be funny, you take a risk that your joke will fail, or even worse, that you will be ridiculed. The very act of telling a joke signals to the group "I am a leader, I can take the risk of failing to be funny, because I am strong—my strength is rooted in being comfortable with my flaws, my vulnerability. Even if this joke fails, I'll still be a leader." In addition, telling a joke demonstrates confidence. A confident person can take risks. A confident person believes in his or her own abilities. You have to take a risk and believe in yourself to tell a joke in front of a crowd. You aren't authentic because your joke succeeded; you are authentic because you thought you had something funny to put forward and were brave enough to let it out.

As for humility, it's beneficial if it's real and detrimental if it's fake. I've experienced both in my working life. What may be surprising is that a genuinely humble leader can get excited about doing something really well and say something ostensibly boastful, such as, "Holy cow, this thing is working now! I actually fixed it! I'm the *man!*" and his or her followers will laugh and know that this guy or gal is as humble as they come.

In contrast, the falsely humble leader would never say anything remotely self-indulgent. He or she may be dedicated to appearing humble, using all the right buzz-words, never using the word *I*, and always talking about *we*. And yet, each of this person's followers, if pressed, would confess to knowing that this leader is merely trying to extract value from appearing humble, rather than being the real thing.

So yes, there are things you can do to appear humble. But if you really think you are God's gift to humanity, and are unwilling to open up and be vulnerable in front of your team, faking it won't work.

How CoachUp Coaches Feel about *Building Connections* with Their Athletes

Among the coaches responding to our CoachUp coaches survey, 100 percent of them feel that having personal relationships with the athletes they coach is important—and most of them (86 percent) feel that it is extremely important. At the beginning of each training session, 94 percent of them greet their athletes with a variety of verbal and physical connections: shaking hands, bumping fists, asking them how it's going, talking about the weather, telling jokes, asking whether there's anything in particular they'd like to work on, and so on.

Eighty-nine percent of CoachUp coaches believe that using humor in their training sessions is either "very effective" or "extremely effective" in connecting with and motivating their athletes to achieve excellence. Interestingly, our coaches find humor just as effective as praise in their training sessions—90 percent of our coaches find tremendous value in using praise liberally to motivate their players. And it's not just private, one-on-one praise that works. In fact, our coaches find it even more valuable to praise their athletes in front of each athlete's parents or in front of other athletes. The most common forms of praise are, in order:

1. Praise the athlete's recent performance in a game or training session
2. Praise the progress he or she has made
3. Acknowledge new skills as he or she masters them, in real time
4. Praise how he or she looks (strong, in good shape, well rested)
5. Relay some good thing the coach has heard about the athlete from another person

And what of criticism? You know—pointing out all the countless mistakes that athletes make in their training sessions? Well, our coaches don't find it all that effective in building connections with their players, with only 50 percent finding it effective in some situations in private settings, and only 27 percent finding it at least somewhat effective in public settings. And when CoachUp coaches do feel a need to offer constructive criticism, the majority do so by:

1. Pointing out exactly what the athlete is doing wrong
2. Explaining and demonstrating how to correct the problem
3. Offering encouraging words

In *Coaching with Heart,* Jerry Lynch sums up what you could characterize as the overwhelming sentiment expressed by top CoachUp coaches from their work with athletes of all levels and abilities: "extraordinary heart-directed coaching begins with one word: relationships, the single most vital aspect to successful coaching."

In each interaction with a player, does your coaching strengthen or weaken that relationship? Are you coaching him or her up, or coaching him or her down? And note, too, that there are times when hard messages— constructive criticism—must be offered through concise direction. But in these situations, does your message hearten or harm your player? How is it delivered? Is the connection strengthened through the honesty and transparency of the message, or does it come off as an attack, the means by which a Showboat coach demonstrates his or her frustration?

Lynch goes on to say: "we are all spiritual beings having an athletic experience, as opposed to athletes and coaches having a spiritual experience. The more I include the whole person in my coaching, the more effective, satisfied, and successful I am."

I think we can all agree that this is the type of coach we would want to play for, whether on the court or in the office.

3

Providing
Genuine Support

"The best business coaches also act as a valuable mirror for their direct reports and help them to better assess what they are doing and how they are doing it."
—John H. Zenger and Kathleen Stinnett,
The Extraordinary Coach: How the Best Leaders Help Others Grow

Okay, what does it mean to give someone genuine support? How does a good coach—or leader, parent, or teacher—support his or her player, colleague, family member, student, or friend? There are lots of ways, big and small, verbal and nonverbal. Basically, providing genuine support comes down to making people feel good, whether about themselves, their performance, their progress, their prospects for the future, or all of these at once. A gift of genuine support is literally *inspiring*—it breathes spirit into the recipient—and *heartening*—it gives them heart, boosts their enthusiasm, and encourages them. Here are some of the ways you can provide genuine support in a Coaching Up Conversation.

Offer Positive Feedback

We all like to hear we're doing well, especially from someone we trust to speak the truth. So tell your player what he or she is doing really well. Be specific, and also be general. If your player has been working on a particular skill and is getting better at it, be sure to mention that you've noticed that improvement and are very impressed by it. If there hasn't been much improvement, but the player is working hard at it, tell your player how much you respect the effort he or she is expending. Praise qualities of character, such as dedication, determination, and guts, as well as progress in individual skills or projects.

In *The Inspiring Leader*, the authors—John H. Zenger, Joseph R. Folkman, and Scott K. Edinger—conducted a study that led them to conclude the following: "Simply put, unless people possess high feelings of confidence or self-efficacy, there simply is no performance. It is too risky, as they see it. Investing your energy is not worth it unless you have a strong belief that you will succeed." It follows that you, as a leader, must do everything in your power to boost the self-esteem of your players.

In basketball, it is common knowledge that a shooter gains confidence, and increases his or her accuracy, after seeing one of his or her shots go through the net. Coaches, competing players, and commentators talk at great length about the importance of preventing a talented scorer from getting easy buckets early in the game. Once that happens, a good scorer tends to heat up. Next time you watch great scorers, such as Stephen Curry or Kevin Durant, play basketball, note how their body language and shot selection changes after they have hit a couple of baskets. Despite being among the best scorers in all of basketball, even they face a mental hurdle at the start of a game. In the back of every scorer's mind is some degree of doubt—"Am I going to have an off night tonight?" So even terrific scorers will do everything they can early on in a game to get some easy baskets or get to the free throw line to make a few free throws. Once they do that, *watch out!* They could end up with a monster night.

The same is true in the workplace. Once someone gains confidence in his or her ability to get things done, he or she starts to look for opportunities to drive results. It's the same mentality good shooters have once they've made a few shots. They will start to look for their next shot, and most important, their teammates will start to look to them and try to find opportunities to get them the ball.

Once you foster an environment in which teammates believe in one another, and are looking for opportunities to assist each other, whether on the court or in the office, your team will take off. Steve Chandler and Scott Richardson write in *100 Ways to Motivate Others*: "I learned that people perform in response to who they think they are for us in the moment. In other words, how we see others is how they perform for us. Once we create a new possibility for those around us, and communicate that to them, their performance as that person instantly takes off." To keep with our analogy, if you help people realize that they are scorers, they will score more for you. The logic holds on any playing field and in any professional field.

But your praise and support have to be genuine. Most people can detect insincerity a mile away. Flattery works only with narcissists; normal people find it uncomfortable. So, tell it like it is. You can always find something truly praiseworthy in another human being.

You can also quote other people. Let your player know that one of his or her teammates or colleagues mentioned how impressed he or she was with your player. In fact, 30 percent of CoachUp coaches go out of their way to relate praise from other people to their athletes—whether it be from their parents, teammates, competitors, or other coaches.

You can give your player positive feedback in private, in a one-on-one conversation, or publicly, in front of his or her teammates, his or her parents, and others. Both ways are valuable. Virtually all the coaches responding to our survey find it highly effective to provide both private and public support for their athletes. Many of them remember in remarkable detail how praise or encouragement from one of their own coaches, early in their athletic careers, made a huge difference in their attitudes and their performance. Here are some representative examples:

"While I was in middle school, my wrestling coach praised one of my skills, and that made me feel great. From then on, I wanted to master more techniques."

"During a film session, my head coach pointed out how well I made a block that allowed us to score. That made a huge impact for me. I played with a lot more vigor."

"My coaches were short on private praise. The thing that heartened me most was overhearing coaches talk to each other about me. After my first scrimmage as a new quarterback, I overheard one coach say to another, 'Well, it looks like we have the quarterback position taken care of.'"

Share a Broader View

Remember that, as a coach, you are likely to have more experience in this arena than your player has. Where he or she may feel stuck or frustrated, you may see progress that he or she hasn't noticed. You may also be able to see potential in your player that he or she has not even imagined, let alone hoped for. Here are some firsthand experiences from our CoachUp coaches of how their own coaches' broader views changed their lives:

"In college I was unsure of myself and didn't have a lot of confidence in my game. But my coach would always talk about how much potential I had. He made me expect more from myself, which helped me to improve as a player. It's important to get the players I work with to have confidence in themselves."

"When I was in college we had a new coach who was firm. He expected a lot out of the throwers and never settled for less than exceptional form. One day when I was struggling during practice I was worried about his reaction. He looked at me and simply said, 'I'm not worried about you. You are a great athlete.' Those words gave me the confidence to keep moving forward. That season I was a nationally ranked javelin thrower and conference champion."

"During a high school football awards banquet, my position coach told the audience that they would be seeing me on Saturdays playing on TV. Prior to that moment, I had never looked past the season or had a goal to play in college. That statement changed everything about how I viewed my athletic future."

"The first thing I tell all my CoachUp clients is the impact private coaching had on me, back when I was taking private lessons in high school. Between my sophomore and junior years I started taking private lessons. During the first session, my coach told me that if I worked hard I could not only play at the college level, but excel there. This comment really had an impact on me, as I hadn't thought much about playing beyond high school at that point. After that, I started looking at the big picture, long term, in how I should approach improving individually on the basketball court. There would be no quick fixes. I would have to work out and practice on my own, knowing that my game wouldn't transform overnight. Over time, I continued to improve. That first private lesson completely changed my outlook. Focusing more on the next level, instead of on just what was in front of me, improved my confidence by leaps and bounds."

Remove Obstacles in Your Player's Path

Remember that your number one job as a coach or leader is to help your player or colleague identify his or her own goals and make progress toward attaining them. Toward that end, you and your player need to be clear about what those goals are, both in the short term and in the longer term. And then one of the ways you support your player is by recognizing and celebrating progress toward those goals, while another is removing obstacles in his or her path. Maybe a teammate or colleague is giving your player a hard time and needs to get set straight. Maybe there are health issues or scheduling issues or family issues that your player is wrestling with, and you can offer counsel or assistance of some kind. Sometimes just listening closely is all the support a person needs in order to feel better about an issue.

On a recent trip to the San Francisco Bay area to visit my uncle, I learned about his grandfather, Sander, the man who made the greatest impact on my uncle's life and after whom one of his own grandsons is named. "What was it about him that made such an impact?" I asked.

He answered, "We would go on fishing trips, and he wouldn't ask me a single thing. If I didn't talk, there would be no talking. He just listened, and responded to what I said. Mainly there was just silence. I learned to be comfortable in my own skin sitting out there on the water. He didn't care if he caught a fish or not, he was just happy to be out on the water with me, being together. I now realize how rare it is to be able to be comfortable with silence, comfortable with being who you are and being present in the moment."

As a coach, sometimes all you have to do is sit next to your player and let him or her talk. Your player will feel your presence, your support, and your openness. Being there, and being present, is an important step in forming an authentic connection. My college basketball coach, Tim Gilbride—"Coach" to all his players—was great at this. Whenever I sat down with him one-on-one, I felt that he wanted me to do the talking. He listened actively. When we were together in a group setting, Coach would never be the center of attention—he would just be among us, laughing along with jokes the guys would tell and taking opportunities to poke fun at guys in his own way. He was really skillful at using humility and humor to reinforce that we were important to him and that he cared about forming and maintaining authentic connections with us. Whether you were a starter or stuck at the end of the bench, Coach would treat you exactly the same. We were all equal in his eyes, and he was one of us, not above us. I think that's why we all cared about him so much and played so hard for him and for each other.

Several years after I graduated, I attended an event honoring his long coaching career. The first thing Coach said when he got up in front of his players, many of whom are now middle-aged guys, was "I'm kind of uncomfortable being up here on this stage, with all this attention on me—I'd much rather be listening to all you guys talk, and having more of a chance to hear what's going on in your lives." And each of us listening to him knew that that was true, because Coach is authentic. He practiced the Coaching Up Model, not only when we played for him, but also in the years that followed. It was always about us, not him. He still cared to connect with us and support us, even way after our playing days ended, and long after he stopped being compensated in any way for offering us direction.

Next time you have a chance at lunchtime, just plop down next to your player and ask, "Okay if I sit with you?" Let your player drive the conversation, or just be present and eat together. Doing that says everything. Really listen, and take time before you respond. Remember to show support first. You will be able to tell when it's the right time, if there is a right time, to offer concise direction.

A few more recollections from CoachUp coaches whose coaches supported them well:

"I was the starting quarterback, but the backup quarterback was very good, and I was insecure about my spot after I heard some kids talking about giving the backup an opportunity. My coach just reassured me that I was his guy, and not to listen to the naysayers."

"I had a coach in high school who was an Olympic trials runner. While he always challenged me to run to the best of my ability, it wasn't until our sectional track meet in the spring that he came up to me with a surprise. He handed me his spikes—the ones he had run the Olympic trials in—and told me he wanted me to wear them for my race. He had never let anyone else wear them before. He joked that the shoes had never run slower than a 4-minute mile (he was an under-4-minute miler) and told me to make sure to keep them that way. That day I ran a 4:11 PR [personal record] and it felt like under 4! He was so proud of me. To this day, more than 35 years later, he was the best coach I ever had."

"At the end of a high school game on the road, my coach came up to me in the locker room and said, 'You completely carried us

on your back tonight. Thank you. We couldn't have won without you.' I realized then how I could take over a game—and how important it was to relax and have fun."

"One of my coaches said that I had made a lot of progress over the summer, and that felt good, because I had spent that whole summer working on my individual game."

"During my first season playing in college, I was not starting. And because I had been injured the season before, my confidence was only so-so. In practice one day, my coach mentioned that he had noticed me improving in defense, and said that I would get the opportunity to play soon. So that encouraged me to continue working hard. Then in a game against our school rivals, one of our defenders got injured. I got the chance to play, and I played really well. After the game, my coach recognized me in front of the team for stepping up to fill in for the injured player, and it gave me confidence to play well the rest of the season as a starter."

But What about Negative Feedback?

"Behavioral studies continue to show that positive reinforcement works more than seven times better than negative criticism to change behavior."
—Steve Chandler and Scott Richardson, *100 Ways to Motivate Others: How Great Leaders Can Produce Insane Results Without Driving People Crazy*

While the CoachUp coaches who responded to our survey were close to unanimous in their shared appreciation for the value of praise in coaching, their views on using criticism or scolding varied considerably. Some of them report that they never use those techniques at all. Of those who do, most prefer to deliver those kinds of messages privately, rather than publicly. And several went out of their way to explain that they always find something to praise before or after offering criticism.

Certainly there are situations in which a coach must convey feedback to a player that will be hard for that player to hear. Negative feedback about performance can still play a supportive role, if the player and coach both understand it as providing an opportunity for improvement. Negative feedback works best if it comes as concise direction, following the formation of an authentic connection and the coach's genuine support of the player.

Here are a couple of typical quotes from CoachUp coaches, reflecting on both their practice with the athletes they are coaching and their own experience as young athletes being coached:

"The only time I ever criticize my athletes is if they are obviously not trying or are being unsafe and are risking hurting themselves or others. It's important to be honest with the athletes. However, I never leave an athlete's lesson without praising them

after criticizing them—and letting their parents know why I criticized them."

"The coaching style that has worked best for me is when a coach acknowledged my effort, before pointing out how fixing something I am doing will elevate my game."

4

Offering Concise Direction

"The mind entertains one thought at a time, and only one. The greatest cause of feeling 'swamped' and 'overwhelmed' in life is . . . not knowing this."
—Steve Chandler and Scott Richardson,
100 Ways to Motivate Others: How Great Leaders Can Produce Insane Results Without Driving People Crazy

The more that you have connected and supported, connected and supported, over and over again, the easier it will be to offer direction. It's like priming the pump. Once you've laid the groundwork and established the relationship, the other person is in a place where he or she is open and trusting and ready to receive the direction.

How do you know when the person is ready? He or she may say: "Coach, tell me what you really want me to work on. Don't hold back."

It's not necessary to authentically connect, genuinely support, and provide concise direction in every conversation. Sometimes you can skip the connection part and move right into supporting and directing. When can you do this? When you have a solid relationship. Think about your best friend. Do you need to start every conversation with a peer-to-peer greeting? No. You can tackle your best friend. You can pull a prank on him. You can greet him pretty much however you like, because your connection is real. Your best friend would likely question whether you are sober if you approached him with a "Hi, Bob, it's so good to see you today. How was your weekend?" What is that? No nicknames? No informality? That's certainly not a very strong friendship.

And even better, you can often skip over both the connection-building and the support-providing parts of the model and jump right to offering the concise direction. Ever asked your best friend for advice on the same thing over and over again? For instance, about a relationship that isn't going well with a significant other? Would your best friend really need to start with "Oh, I'm so glad you asked me, I'm happy to provide some guidance here. You know I'm here for you, and care about you a lot" and then provide support with a "I know this must be hard for you. You are a great person and you care about her feelings, so I'm sure this isn't easy"? No, your best friend would likely say, "Dude, are you kidding me? For the hundredth time, you need to dump her, it's totally unacceptable that she cheated on you with your brother!" Boom. There's the concise direction without any need for reconfirming a connection or offering support; your friend knows those things are firmly in place.

My first year playing professional basketball in Israel, I played for Hapoel Migdal Jerusalem—the beloved professional basketball team of the city of Jerusalem and one of the best teams not only in Israel's top league, but also in all of European international competition. I had been a leading (all-league, all-state, all–New England, etc.) player the previous year as a senior at Bowdoin College, helping guide the team to the best year in school history. But that was Division III collegiate basketball. Making the jump from that level of play to being a rookie on one of the best professional basketball teams in the world was quite a leap. My new team included six former National Basketball Association (NBA) players and four Israeli National Team players. I was the eleventh player. At

6'6", and having normally played as a power forward, I arrived in Israel with an image of myself as a big guy. Well, on Hapoel Jerusalem we had a 7-footer—and he played as our starting *small forward*. I quickly realized that this was another level of the sport I loved. I was buried on the bench and relegated to rookie chores—carrying the veterans' bags on all our team flights to Europe and Russia for international competition and essentially serving as a practice player.

Nonetheless, my coach, Israeli basketball legend Guy Goodes, saw something in me, and to my great surprise he signed me to a multiyear contract. When Coach David Blatt left our number one rival, Maccabi Tel Aviv, two years ago to become the head coach of the NBA's Cleveland Cavaliers, helping them reach the NBA championship with LeBron James in 2014–2015, it was Guy Goodes who replaced David Blatt as the head coach of Maccabi Tel Aviv. Needless to say, we are talking about an elite level of basketball here and an elite coach in Guy Goodes, who himself had been a longtime star as a player with Maccabi Tel Aviv and the Israeli National Team back in his day.

Like any great coach, Coach Goodes excelled at defining roles. He made my role very clear to me: (1) I was to push our star power forward, Omar Sneed, in practice (except on game days or when we were traveling, we had two tough 2-hour practices a day), and (2) I was to help bridge the division between the American and Israeli players in the locker room. That was it. This was a year for me to learn, to develop as a player, and to support the team in the locker room and at practice.

When we signed Roger Powell, Jr., a 6′6″ former standout forward, who helped take the University of Illinois team to the National Collegiate Athletic Association (NCAA) finals and who later played with the NBA's Seattle Supersonics, Utah Jazz, and Chicago Bulls, his addition to our team caused a lot of concern in the locker room. First, a very well-liked player was released from our roster to make room for Roger, and second: *Roger was really good!* Although he came off the bench, his addition posed a threat to the playing time of our other star forwards. As for me, well, I was hardly playing anyway; but the addition of Roger meant that I would surely never see the court that year.

So, what did Coach Goodes ask me to do? He solicited my opinion on what we could do as a team to help Roger adjust to life in Israel and be more connected to the team. So I set about making a concerted effort to look out for Roger. After all, I knew firsthand how difficult it could be for a new arrival to get adjusted to a foreign country and a new team. I spent a lot of time taking Roger out to eat, showing him new places, introducing him to new people, and rooming together and hanging out together while we traveled to Europe and Russia for our away games. When we broke up into pairs to shoot jump shots at practice, I was assigned to work with Roger. Roger, being an amazing person, made the job particularly fun, despite never letting me outshoot him.

By further involving me in the overall success of the team, Coach Goodes both provided genuine support for Roger through me and gave my role on the team purpose. My identity that year—as a guy who might not be playing in the games but who could help the team through his presence in the locker room and his efforts in practice—was reinforced by Coach Goodes's support for my role.

After all, many of the players on any team don't play starring roles but supporting roles, as I did on Hapoel Jerusalem. How do you, as a coach, effectively engage and integrate everyone on the team? So often, coaches focus their attention and praise on the stars, causing the other players to feel left out. Almost all of us, as athletes, have known that feeling of not being the apple of the coach's eye, and it negatively affects our motivation and cohesion as a team. What Coach Goodes did to empower both Roger and me was a powerful lesson in providing indirect support for the players on your team, regardless of their roles.

And how did Coach Goodes provide concise direction? I remember having a really good scrimmage against Hapoel Holon. It was the most playing time I had all season, even though it didn't count as an official game. I matched up against Deron Washington, a star 6'7" small forward who had been a second-round NBA pick by the Detroit Pistons the previous year out of Virginia Tech. Let's put it this way: Deron was much, much better than me at basketball. There will never be any point, no matter how many years go by, at which I will ever be as good as Deron. He was an elite athlete who could run by me and jump over me at will.

But I played really well that game. I hit my shots, made some good plays, and did a decent job defending him. I wouldn't say I outplayed him that game, but I held my own. It was a huge boost to my self-esteem as a player, having played at a small college and not yet sure whether I really belonged in a top professional league. After the game, I had a new belief in myself as a capable role player at the professional level. So I was feeling pretty good about my performance after the game, with the exception of having missed one of my free throws. As I was making my way out of the arena, I ran into Coach Goodes. I must have smiled at him, because he smiled back. And there it was—and I was waiting for it—some genuine support, please, Coach! "Hey, kid," he said, "nice job. But next time, make your damn free throws." We both laughed.

What was his message? "Get off it, Jordan. You played okay. Don't get too caught up in it, because you have a long way to go. But enjoy the moment." If he weren't authentic, if he weren't a real coach—someone who played the game at a high level, who really understood what was going through the mind of his young player, and who really got it—he wouldn't have said anything at all, or maybe he would have just said, "Good game." Instead, he reinforced that despite him being the coach, and me the lowly rookie destined for many more months on the bench and likely a long-term career in something other than professional basketball, there was a mutual respect. It made me excited to carry out the role he assigned me that year, despite the frustrations of being on the low end of the totem pole.

And that's exactly the point: by being a transparent leader—one who displays humor and humility, who assigns clear roles, strives to foster transparency throughout the organization, and provides genuine support—a coach earns the right to lead.

And this is really important: *the best coaches and leaders are able to get so much done, in so little time, in communicating what they need of their players in crunch time conversations precisely because they can skip over steps 1 and 2 and cut right to the chase.* Their players want that direction and are in a position to receive it positively and act on it enthusiastically, because they know from numerous previous interactions that they have an authentic connection with their coach and that their coach genuinely supports them and wants what's best for them.

I was receptive to Coach Goodes's very concise direction to me, "Make your damn free throws," because we had an authentic connection and because he not only provided genuine support to my teammates and me but also literally defined my role as one in which I would spend my entire season supporting my other teammates in practice, in the locker room, and on the road. It was very clear to all of us that what motivated Coach was the team's success. If the team did well, then we would each benefit individually as professional players. Toward that end, he supported us, and he asked that we support one another.

So we did. I'll never forget how tight we became as a team. Despite having not seen one another for many years, I know that we would all drop everything to help one another to this day. Adam Haluska, Travis Watson, Timmy Bowers, Omar Sneed, Torin Francis, and, of course, Roger Powell—we were a hell of a team. I give Coach Goodes all the credit in the world for being able to successfully merge those talented American players with our terrific Israeli National Team stars—Yuval Naimy, Moran Roth, Sharon Shason, and Erez Marckovich. The brotherhood and strength of those relationships remains as strong as ever to this day.

It takes a transformational leader to unite a highly talented, highly competitive, and socially and culturally disparate group. It takes a whole set of skills at listening well, building authentic connections, providing genuine support, and offering concise direction to help each individual see the bigger picture. When we were on our game, we were almost unstoppable as we demonstrated at home against our archrival Maccabi Tel Aviv, winning easily against the best team in the Euroleague at that time.

When you are part of a special group, going after a big mission, led by a leader who practices the Coaching Up Model, you dedicate yourself to the team and become fully invested in the outcome. The few truly outstanding teams I've been on—my senior year Bowdoin College basketball team, my rookie year Hapoel Jerusalem pro basketball team, and the team we forged at CoachUp during our first few years getting the company off the ground—those tight-knit teams were amazing to be a part of. It didn't matter whether my role was as a leading player (Bowdoin), a rookie on the bench (Jerusalem), or the CEO/founder/coach (CoachUp). Though each team was as different from the others as you might think possible, they all shared the same set of values, passed down from leaders who practiced the Coaching Up Model. And the results speak for themselves—each team won, and won big.

Have you ever seen Coach K at Duke, perhaps the best coach on the planet, turn bright red and yell at his players in the heat of a game? Do you think his players are offended? Do you think they shrivel up inside and want to crawl back to their dorm rooms and hide from the world? No! They know Coach K is real—and is there for them. Coach K has done the legwork, starting with the recruiting process, the practice sessions, the film room studies, the bus rides, and all the hundreds of interactions with his players, to prepare precisely for that moment—the moment when the outcome of the big game hinges on his ability to communicate clearly and effectively with his players, without them feeling that they are being *coached down*. As Shane Battier puts it:

"What makes Coach K better than any other coach in the entire world, in any sport, is his ability to understand every member of his team and what makes each of them tick. It's his ability to unite and inspire the whole group, by connecting with and inspiring each of us in his own special way. That's an unbelievable skill. I have no doubt that if Coach K weren't the world's greatest basketball coach, he'd be running a Fortune 500 company, or he'd be a senator, a great general, or pretty much anything he wanted to be. He just has an uncanny ability to *reach* the people in his circle. In terms of the Coaching Up Model, he's a genius at building authentic connections."

If you get great players, the rest has a way of taking care of itself. If you have star players, who respect you as a coach, work hard, play unselfishly, and lead by example, other top recruits will self-select to play for your program, and your star players will hold the rest accountable to a higher purpose of supporting the team and prioritizing winning above all else. And everyone (rookies included!) will fall into line.

In *The Extraordinary Coach*, the authors John H. Zenger and Kathleen Stinnett describe the importance of establishing a caring, trusting relationship between a leader and a follower before anything can get accomplished:

"Very few individuals shared that they valued the coaching they received from leaders with whom they had a rocky relationship. . . . Most of the time, the number one attribute provided is 'My coach genuinely cared about me.' A trust-based relationship must be in place if coaching is to work."

Ways to Offer Concise Direction

There are many ways to offer concise direction. Four of the best are these: directly, indirectly, Socratically, and circuitously.

Directly: "Remember that 'down up' move we worked on, where you lead with the left jab, then fake another one, but land with the straight right? Do that." Or, my personal favorite, "Make your damn free throws."

Indirectly: Sometimes you can offer a general comment that allows the other person to come up with a suggestion of his or her own. This is ideal, because then he or she owns the direction. You can heartily endorse it, repeating it back to the other person, perhaps inviting an exploration of next steps, setting specific targets, identifying possible or anticipated obstacles, formulating tactics and strategies, and so on.

"Man, it would be great if we could find some way to better pressure their point guard as he brings the ball up the floor. Their backup point guard isn't playing today, so their starter has to go the distance, and he's going to get tired in the fourth quarter if we pressure him. Hmm . . ."

"Sure, Coach, I have an idea. Let me pick him up full court and make him work." Now you have the player coming up with the correct direction. This is the best possible outcome. When the direction comes from your player, it increases his or her buy-in to making the outcome successful. After all, it was the player's idea!

Socratically: another way to offer direction is by asking carefully shaped questions: "what do you think might happen if we played you and Sarah in the post? I'd love to get you on the court for 10 more minutes; how do you think we could do that without hurting our transition defense?"

"Well, I would need to get in better shape to prove to you I can handle the extra minutes. Let me make that my goal this month." Now the player is taking responsibility for a plan that will enable a future additional lineup option.

If it doesn't happen, then let some time go by and pick it back up again. "Hey Alex, you mind hanging with me for a few? I wanted to run something by you . . . Do you remember that conversation we had about playing you and Sarah in the post? Yes? Well, maybe now is a good time to revisit that. Are you ready for playing some time at power forward in the coming weeks? Is your conditioning good enough to play 30 minutes full speed, or should I pace your minutes to keep you fresh for the fourth quarter, when we really need you to close out the game?"

Circuitously: although it's almost always better to go directly to a player, under some circumstances, it may prove useful to go through one of his or her teammates. For instance, my college coach noticed that one of my good friends on the team, and fellow co-captain, seemed depressed. Coach wasn't sure what was going on with him, but he clearly wasn't himself. He expressed concern for my buddy as a person first and as his player second, and asked me whether I had noticed the same thing. I told him, "His grandmother just passed away, Coach. They were very close. He'll be okay, but it hit him pretty hard." This info allowed my coach to figure out the best path forward in helping my talented teammate play through that emotional pain.

By the way, why did I feel okay about offering Coach that information? Because we had an authentic connection, because he had genuinely supported me, and because I knew he did the same with all his players. I knew Coach was asking me because he wanted to be respectful of my teammate. Very likely he thought that approaching him about it directly might not be the best course of action, in case my teammate didn't want to open up, which would have caused an awkward situation. If Coach hadn't understood and practiced the Coaching Up Model, he likely never would have asked me about my teammate, and even if he had, I probably would have kept my mouth shut.

See, a coach who chooses to *coach up*, instead of *coaching down*, gets so much more out of his or her players. And best of all, the Coaching Up Model enables coaches who practice it to be even better at the job. Moreover, this approach isn't limited to sports, business, and the home. Can you imagine a general who doesn't ask his officers on the ground for their opinion on the battle as it progresses? Or even worse, a general who is not respected and trusted by his troops, and from whom they withhold information? How could that general make good decisions? How could that general even be in a position to offer good, concise direction in a crunch?

5

Making It Work
at Work

"*Much has been said about why people leave their organizations. The cliché has emerged that people don't quit the company, they quit their boss. Our research confirms that the boss has an enormous impact on how people behave and whether they stay or leave the organization.*"
—John H. Zenger, Joseph R. Folkman, and
Scott K. Edinger, *The Inspiring Leader:
Unlocking the Secrets of How Extraordinary
Leaders Motivate*

"*The manager traditionally holds the paycheck, the key to promotion, and also the axe. This is fine so long as you believe that the only way to motivate is through the judicious application of the carrot and the stick. However, for coaching to work at its best the relationship between the coach and the coachee must be one partnership in the endeavor, of trust, of safety, and of minimal pressure. The check, the key, and the axe have no place here, as they can only serve to inhibit such a relationship."*

—John Whitmore, *Coaching for Performance: GROWing Human Potential and Purpose: The Principles and Practice of Coaching and Leadership*

Most adults between the ages of 18 and 68 spend some 35 percent of their waking hours in the workplace. That's a huge chunk of time by any standard. So, the quality of that time—how comfortable we are at work, how motivated we are to engage in the task at hand, how effective we feel, and how satisfied we are with the results we achieve—will clearly have a major impact on who we are and how we feel about ourselves. And as indicated in the above quote, studies have confirmed that the single most important factor determining a person's sense of well-being in the workplace is the quality of the relationship that person has with his or her "boss."

I need to mention here that I really loathe the word *boss*. In my view, there should be no such word in the vocabulary of an enlightened organization. Sure, businesses need structure, and it does make sense to have somebody take responsibility for guiding groups of people who are working together to get things done. But why call those folks *bosses*? *Boss* connotes bossiness, and who can tolerate that?

But of course, while the words we use matter a lot, the issues affecting workplaces these days run far deeper than nomenclature. As Christine Porath and Christine Pearson point out in "The Price of Incivility": "rudeness at work is rampant, and it's on the rise. Over the past 14 years we've polled thousands of workers about how they're treated on the job and 98 percent have reported experiencing uncivil behavior. In 2011 half said they were treated rudely at least once a week—up from a quarter in 1998."

The sad truth is that just as there are still Showboat sports coaches who coach their players down, rather than up, so too there are Showboat business executives who like to throw their weight around. We are all familiar with the caricature of a boss as egomaniacal, imperious, and abrupt to the point of rudeness: in short, bossy. This kind of executive treats colleagues like pieces of office furniture, or perhaps indentured servants, whose job is to make him or her happy. As a result, everyone who reports to this kind of executive endures a constant state of depression, anxiety, and dread.

Unfortunately, this Showboat style of business leadership is still widely prevalent in all kinds of organizations, from fledgling startups all the way up to Fortune 500 companies. Maybe they're not all quite as bad as the caricature sketched above; stereotypes generally exaggerate, after all. But a huge number of business executives still lean heavily in that direction. I bet you've run up against at least a few of them in your own career. For that kind of *boss*, everything is all about him or her. He or she needs to meddle in everyone else's work, micromanaging and finding fault. These people excuse this kind of behavior by saying, "Hey, my number one priority is to make profits for our shareholders; I have to oversee every detail to make sure it's done right—and I don't have time for any touchy-feely stuff." Or, "Hey, I'm dealing with adults here; if they can't take orders and get the job done the way I want it done, I'll find someone who can."

As it happens, this swaggering, self-focused, "my way or the highway" approach to business leadership misses the mark, not just because it's insensitive and crude, but also—and even more important—because it just doesn't work. This approach to managing people fails for the same reasons that the Showboat approach to coaching fails: because, as we mentioned earlier, force-feeding doesn't nourish, shouting doesn't communicate, and humiliation doesn't inspire. People who are coached down shut down. Anxiety and resentment consume their energy and kill their creativity.

So Showboat executives are doing a huge disservice not only to their colleagues but also to their enterprises. Very likely their narcissistic approach to managing their colleagues is significantly damaging the organization's productivity—and cutting into the very profits the Showboat executive is so concerned about. That executive will never know what it feels like to see his or her colleagues throw their whole selves enthusiastically into their projects, working creatively and passionately because they feel valued and because they have been helped to understand how their own interests and goals align with those of the organization.

Understanding now the overwhelming case in favor of the power and principles of the Coaching Up Model, as opposed to coaching down, what additional practical steps can we take to maximize the effectiveness and efficiency of our coaching practice in the workplace?

Revisiting the Pareto Principle

Let's take a fresh look at the Pareto Principle, also known as the 80/20 rule. You're probably already familiar with this rule, which was formulated by Vilfredo Pareto (1848–1923), an Italian economist-sociologist who was a professor of political economy in Lausanne, Switzerland. His principle has become a widely used tool in organizational and business management, among many other fields. Basically, it suggests that very often in human endeavors there is a wide disparity between input and output, generally with a ratio of 80 to 20 (though the ratios can be quite different, and the two parts of the ratio don't need to add up to 100).

For instance, a manufacturing company may invest 20 percent of its resources in putting out a product that yields a whopping 80 percent of its revenues, while another 80 percent of its resources go toward products that together generate just 20 percent of its revenues. Clearly, it may be a good idea to expand that more profitable item in the company's product line and reduce or cancel at least some of the less profitable items.

Similarly, as business leaders and workers we often spend 80 percent of our workday on things that deserve only 20 percent of our energy and attention, and vice versa. The key to working effectively is allocating our focus and efforts so that the things we care about most get most of our energy and attention. This principle holds true for people working at every level of every organization. It just makes sense, right? But how often do we really think about it and ensure that we're following that principle in our work lives?

So the question for every business executive is this: how important is it to you to have the people in your organization or group truly aligned with its goals and enthusiastic about pursuing their careers within it? If the answer to that question is "very important" (as I hope and trust that it is), then what percentage of your time are you spending to ensure that your colleagues fit that description? That is, how much of your attention is focused on hiring great people, building authentic relationships with them, providing genuine support to them, and offering them concise direction? I hope the answer to that second question is a resounding "most of my time" or even "almost all my time." But if that's not the answer you come up with, then it's time to think deeply about your priorities and rejigger your calendar.

Let's take a lesson from the great Coach K at Duke: all that time he spent recruiting, connecting with, and supporting Shane Battier and other brilliant players, he

wasn't diagramming plays with *x*s and *o*s on a clipboard.
Coaches at the highest levels of any sport know that the
most critically important part of their work is all about
getting terrific players and then connecting with them,
supporting them, and motivating them.

The same principle holds for businesses. Leading an
enterprise, or a portion of one, shouldn't be much about
all those tactical decisions. You're far better off hiring
people who are really great—in fact, people who are
better than you at what they do—and then getting out of
their way and letting them make those tactical decisions.
In *100 Ways to Motivate Others*, Steve Chandler and Scott
Richardson describe the importance of team building
above all else: "the best managers we have ever trained
always took more time and trouble in the hiring process
than any of their competitors did. Then, once they hired
ambitious people, they based their management on the
management of those people's personal goals. These
managers were spending their days managing results,
not activities. Their positive reinforcement was always
for results, not for activities."

So, it makes sense that where executives should spend
80 percent of their time, just like college coaches, is on
recruiting, connecting with, and supporting their players.
The other 20 percent should be spent on the tactical part
of the job—what in sports I call *active coaching*. This has to
do with which person you put in which job and how you

define and measure what he or she is doing. In work situations, as in sports situations, the more you do of the connecting and supporting, the less you need to do of the other stuff.

Remember, too, that when you are actively coaching it is at least as important, if not more important, to be in command of your mood as of the actual direction you offer. In "The Price of Incivility," Christine Porath and Christine Pearson note: "when talking about leaders' moods, the importance of resonance cannot be over-stated. While our research suggests that leaders should generally be upbeat, their behavior must be rooted in realism, especially when faced with crisis."

Adopting a Truly Transformative Mental Model

In addition to looking at your time through the double lens of the Pareto Principle and the Coaching Up Model, you may find it hugely useful to make a profound shift in how you view each colleague and each conversation. That shift involves moving from purely transactional perspectives and conversations, which are short term in focus and all about getting a specific task done, to transformational perspectives and conversations, which are longer term in focus and more open to the possibility of doing things differently and better.

For instance, discussing the way a colleague is handling a particular project this week is transactional; exploring with that colleague ways that the company might orchestrate a more effective way of handling all such projects, or whether that project is even a priority in the first place, could be transformational.

By the same token, it's important to be thinking about colleagues not as fixed in their current positions but as people who likely have aspirations to grow in their work and assume additional responsibilities. Your water cooler conversations with colleagues you view in this way might involve more open-ended questions, something like this: "hey, George, how was the weekend? What'd you do? And hey, I heard you did a great job last week on X, well done. And where are you thinking of taking it next?"

Open, exploratory conversations of that kind are probably the most important activity taking place among colleagues. Certainly they yield more stimulating and valuable results than purely transactional conversations. It's worth noting that when you lead this way, you are actively pushing yourself to a higher standard, as much as you are providing for others. The Mandarin Chinese concept of *Jingshen* well defines the impact you can have on others when you practice the Coaching Up Model—the concept translates as "instilling vitality, passion, spirit and individual power in those you lead."

Matters of Leadership Style and Behavior

If we put everything we do as business leaders under the lens of the Coaching Up Model, how does it fit? Or to look at it a bit differently, if we consider how everything we do might be taken by our employees, how might we change our behavior?

One of the fundamental issues that any company faces is deciding what style of office organization it will adopt. When I founded CoachUp, Inc., I realized that one of the things that really mattered to me was modeling our culture after the most effective sports teams that I had participated in as a player and coach. I wanted an environment in which people felt comfortable and happy coming to work and knew they were equal members of the team, regardless of their roles or prior experience.

For instance, having a private office with a door that closes, when others are out in the open, says, "I'm above you, I'm better than you." Do you really need that private office? I naturally wanted an office where everyone could see one another pulling together. I wanted it to feel like a locker room. And so we set it up that way—from an open layout with everyone sitting together at long tables, to sports team memorabilia, and yes, even old high school lockers for people to keep their personal belongings in. Now, of course, this setup was appropriate in part because my company is involved in sports. But after working this way for years, I would encourage the same setup for any company, because the most effective organizations are those that feel like high-functioning sports teams. It's great to see a shift in this direction taking place over the last five years. In many companies nowadays, especially nimble young startups and high-tech companies, everyone, at all levels, sits comfortably together in large, open spaces, with a few meeting rooms available for anyone to use when private conversations are necessary.

And how about the company dress code? Do your top executives wear more formal clothes than their colleagues? Do they sit in better chairs, at bigger desks? What does that say to your colleagues? On sports teams, we would all dress pretty much the same. It was about being comfortable. What was important to us was staying flexible, maintaining proper hydration, and getting enough sleep. We would also, proudly, wear our team's name and logo whenever possible. I remember feeling proud to be on the men's varsity basketball team in college and to wear our team's sweatshirts around campus. And one of my proudest moments was after signing my first professional basketball contract with Hapoel Jerusalem—the first thing they did when the paperwork was finalized was to hand me a big bag full of team-branded clothing, which I pretty much lived in all year long. At CoachUp, I made it a priority from the early days that we fostered an environment in which people could wear whatever made them comfortable. And whenever possible we made available, and encouraged people to wear, CoachUp-branded clothing.

What about your terminology as a leader? In introducing a colleague to someone else, do you say, "He/she works for me," or do you say, "We work together, we're on the same team"? Do you say, "I'm his/her manager" or "We're colleagues"?

Does the senior executive in your organization lay out a plan with each of his or her direct reports, explaining how their current jobs and their trajectories may affect their later careers? Have you yourself, as the leader of your organization or group, expressed interest in each person working with you and his or her goals for his or her whole career? Have you explained to your colleagues how their current jobs might help them move in those desired directions? Conducting these conversations may cost you a few minutes on a busy day, but they're likely to yield huge results in terms of your colleagues' motivation.

After attending a board meeting or a high-level executive meeting, do you sit down with your whole team and take them through what was discussed so that they all understand how their work aligns with the organization's goals? And during such meetings and other conversations with high-ranking colleagues, do you give your teammates full credit for their contributions to whatever progress your team may have achieved, or do their names never come up?

Regularly Scheduled Meetings with Colleagues

Many leaders have the misconception that every coaching session has to be 50 minutes long. It need not be that way. Some topics may need only 15 or 20 minutes.

—John H. Zenger and Kathleen Stinnett,
The Extraordinary Coach: How the Best Leaders Help Others Grow

How often does each executive at your organization have a one-on-one session with each of his or her direct reports? At CoachUp we do it weekly, generally for an hour. But unfortunately, as John Zenger and Kathleen Stinnett go on to point out, "Most managers will conclude that approximately 85–90 percent of the time (in their one-on-one meetings with direct reports) is concerned with project or task status updates."

When you think about conducting a 1-hour session with each of your own colleagues in terms of the Coaching Up Model, how would you structure that hour? The model suggests that most of your focus should be on connection and support.

Even if the topic under discussion is tactical, you should find a way to weave in connection and support. Use your body language. Lean in, turn off the phone, accept no interruptions, and support the job your colleague is doing. Ask about any frustrations and impediments; then work with him or her to try to come up with some solutions. "How can I help?" is a great question. Focus on connection and support, and view your role as one in which, via concise direction, you are able to remove bottlenecks for your direct report. Remember that you are the coach, and it's your role—your most important role—to coach your player up.

In the renowned leadership book *Crucial Conversations*, the authors (Kerry Patterson, Joseph Grenny, Ron McMillan, and Al Switzler) articulate well the importance of opening the door for transparent conversations and genuine support: "at the core of every successful conversation lies the free flow of relevant information. People openly and honestly express their opinions, share their feelings, and articulate their theories."

And underlying all such conversations is the essential human faculty of empathy—or "feeling with" another person. In "What Makes a Leader?" Daniel Goleman underscores the value of empathy in the workplace: "of all the dimensions of emotional intelligence, empathy is the most easily recognized. We all have felt the empathy of a sensitive teacher or friend; we have all been struck by its absence in an unfeeling coach or boss. But when it comes to business, we rarely hear people praised, let alone rewarded for their empathy. The very word seems unbusinesslike, out of place amid the tough realities of the marketplace."

Why are we not hiring for empathy, looking out for it, training for it, and rewarding it?

A good question, isn't it?

6

Taking It Home to the Family

"Children are not a distraction from more important work. They are the most important work."

—John Trainer, MD

"The problem with parent-child management is that the person being managed does not feel respected in the exchange. And the most important, the most powerful, precondition to good performance is trust and respect."

—Steve Chandler and Scott Richardson,
100 Ways to Motivate Others: How Great Leaders Can Produce Insane Results Without Driving People Crazy

When we think of applying the Coaching Up Model within the family, it's natural to think first of parents applying the model in raising their kids. After all, parents are constantly guiding their offspring, pretty much from birth through the day they take those first wobbly steps, head off nervously to that first day of school, learn the principles of tying shoelaces and fair play and taking turns, acquire table manners, and remember to look both ways at street corners, right up through the maelstrom of adolescence and borrowing the family car. Along the way, the opportunities for building an authentic connection, providing genuine support, and offering concise direction are almost infinite.

But parents are not the only family members who have a wealth of opportunities to coach other family members up. Children as young as four or five years old can often be observed offering counsel to their siblings—especially if they have benefited from wise and kind coaching themselves, whether from their parents or from older siblings, grandparents, aunts, uncles, or cousins. And, of course, as children grow into adulthood, their aging parents are increasingly likely to turn to them for counsel—as well as to their own parents and siblings. The more a family practices the principles of coaching one another up, the longer the habit of Coaching Up Conversations is likely to last among them, and to get handed down from generation to generation.

It's important to note, too, that families come in many shapes and sizes: single-parent families; two-parent families; multiple-parent/stepparent/grandparent/step-grandparent families; families led by aunts, uncles, or neighbors; families who live in one apartment or in multiple houses or who share their living space with other families. Some of the examples and anecdotes in this chapter may feel more relevant to some families than to others. But it's my firm conviction that people in all these kinds of families can benefit from adopting the principles and practices embedded in the Coaching Up Model and making them their own.

If you are a parent reading this chapter—or if you are embedded in a family of any kind, whether you are a parent or not—you may feel that you and your fellow family members are already pretty adept at using all three aspects of the Coaching Up Model: building an authentic connection, providing genuine support, and offering concise direction. And, of course, you may be right; you may already be doing all those fine things in virtually every interaction you have with your partner, kids, siblings, parents, grandparents, aunts, uncles, or cousins.

But if, in your heart of hearts, you suspect that there may be some room for improvement in your family's communications and relationships, let's run through the Coaching Up Model one more time. By focusing specifically on applying the model consciously and continuously in our family life, we can strengthen family bonds,

---

smooth difficult conversations, and free up a whole lot of joyful energy.

A Coaching Up Conversation with a Child

Sometimes it's hard to remember, in the heat of an angry moment, how deeply we love the person we're angry with. This is particularly true of kids, who have not yet learned that it's possible to love someone and be angry with him or her at the same time.

An enraged six-year-old may scream at his mother, "You are SO MEAN! I HATE YOU!" And his mother, who has just saved the family dog's life by grabbing out of the child's hand the 16-ounce bag of chocolate chips the child was about to pour into the dog's dish, may be tempted to shout right back with similar sentiments or to silence the child or punish him in some other way—any of which would only make the child even angrier. It may require all the mother's willpower to recall that the child was not *trying* to kill the dog.

Ideally, she will have the presence of mind to take a deep breath, let it out slowly, and respond calmly, looking the boy right in the eyes. The conversation may go something along these lines:

> MOM: I see that you're feeling pretty angry right now, aren't you?

BOY nods, mute, enraged.

MOM: And I'm sorry you're feeling that way, because that's not a very happy way to feel, is it?

BOY shakes his head no.

MOM: But I couldn't let you feed Jake those chocolate chips. Do you know why?

BOY shakes his head no again, still mad, but interested.

MOM: Because dogs' stomachs are different from ours, and chocolate is very bad and dangerous for them. Chocolate can even *kill* a dog.

BOY, wide-eyed in surprise: Really?

MOM, moving closer to him and taking him in her arms: I love you very much, and I love Jake, too, just like you love him. And I know you want to take good care of him and make him happy, right?

BOY, nodding, relieved: Right.

MOM: And you didn't know about chocolate being dangerous for dogs. But now you do know, okay? So now, if anybody else wants to give chocolate to Jake, or to any other dog, what will you do?

BOY: I'll make them stop!

MOM: Wonderful! You'll be a fine protector for Jake, and for other dogs, too.

BOY: I'll be like Superman.

MOM: Right! And now, if you still feel like giving Jake a treat, why don't you give him one of his dog biscuits? And then how about if you and I take him outside to play catch for a while, and later you can help me brush him and feed him his dinner? Does that sound like a good plan?

BOY, enthusiastically: Yes!

MOM: But first, how about a hug?

BOY and MOM hug.

What has happened here? The mother has:

- addressed the angry child calmly and affectionately, modeling a mature way to react to another person's anger
- offered him a label naming his feeling, shifting his understanding of his own feeling from hatred to anger
- supported him by emphasizing that his negative feeling is something happening *right now*, not something permanent; he will not always feel this way
- respected him by recognizing the goodness of his underlying motivation, to make their pet happy
- confirmed that she knows he was innocent of any intention to harm their pet
- taught him useful information about the dangers of chocolate for dogs

- reaffirmed that she loves him
- inspired him to take on a new, empowered role as a protector of dogs
- offered him concise direction about three healthy ways to make his pet happy in the immediate future
- offered him her companionship in the latter activities and the warmth of a hug

This is a fine model of a Coaching Up Conversation between a parent and a child. I'm betting that child was quite happy giving Jake that treat, taking him outside to play catch, and helping his mother brush him and feed him his dinner. The boy was fulfilling his original, generous impulse to make his pet happy, and his mother, despite having swiftly repossessed (and no doubt prudently hidden) those chocolate chips, used the occasion to coach him up, not down. The child learned that it was okay to express his anger, that he hadn't actually meant it about hating his mother, that he could trust his mother to understand and love him even when he made a mistake, and that life as he knew it would go on happily despite a momentary spasm of anger.

So, let's revisit the three basic elements in the Coaching Up Model in the specific context of the family: building an authentic connection, providing genuine support, and offering concise direction.

Building an Authentic Connection

Okay, this one should be a piece of cake within a family, right? We are all programmed to bond with other members of our family, clan, or tribe. A baby born into a healthy family just naturally gets the warmest welcome in the world. The baby barely fidgets and food appears. He or she begins to practice smiling, and all the big faces around him or her smile back and coo with delight. The baby's parent or parents, grandparents, aunts, uncles, and even older siblings (although this can be complicated and can take a while) typically fall utterly in love with this miraculous little person.

So deep, reciprocal bonding takes place, and it's wonderful. But then as the baby gets older and more mobile and independent, other forces come into that loving relationship. The baby's parents are stressed and tired, torn among their various responsibilities—to the baby and his or her siblings, to their work, to their own parents, and to their friends and colleagues. There is never enough time or energy. Frictions arise and must be dealt with. As children grow they may have tantrums, get into fights, break family rules, and worry their parents sick. Tempers sometimes flare, and harsh words are spoken.

And, of course, lots of times those things don't happen. The kids head off happily to school, come happily home, play enthusiastically with their friends, and generally are entirely cheerful, charming, cooperative, and delightful family members. Even so, there is still the danger that the family's deep, authentic connections—between the parents, between parents and children, and among the children—may fray or fade for any number of reasons. Familiarity can indeed breed contempt—or, more commonly, complacency. We're all so busy multitasking; it's easy to lose sight of what's most important.

Perhaps the strongest threat to our authentic connection with every member of our family is that we get lulled into taking one another for granted. We assume that because we love one another well and truly, that's enough. It's easy to forget that every one of us is always a work in progress. The young child we sing to sleep with the same song every night will suddenly be heading off to first grade and not want that song anymore, and we've missed something along the way.

How can we keep in close touch with all the members of our families and never, ever take our connections with them for granted? Maintaining vivid, authentic connections is mostly a matter of daily practice. Ask yourself these questions:

1. When you or your partner, parent, sibling, or child leaves for school or work, how do you say good-bye? What kind of contact do you have—physical, verbal, and emotional?

2. Whenever you are reunited with your partner, parent, sibling, or child, even after a few hours apart, how do you greet each other? Again, what kind of physical, verbal, and emotional contact do you have?
3. In the evening, how do you say good night to each other? Are there hugs, kisses, bedtime stories, songs, rituals, or at least a sincere "sweet dreams"?
4. Do you regularly sit down together as a family—perhaps around the dinner table—and check in with one another, to see what each family member is working on or thinking about?
5. If a family member asks for your time—whether to throw a ball around, help with a homework assignment, talk about a problem he or she is having, or whatever—how do you respond? Can you take a leaf from Big Ed Battier's book and at least make an effort to always be willing to engage?
6. When you talk with a family member, does he or she always have your undivided attention? Do you have a family rule, as Coach K has with the players on his team at Duke, that if you have something to say, you look the other person in the eyes while you say it? Sure, it's fine to chat amiably while doing something side by side—maybe chopping vegetables for dinner or working together in the garden. Such activities can be great bonding opportunities, too. But whenever something personal or significant comes up, it's important to put down whatever

you're doing and give your partner/child/sibling your undivided attention.

Of course, the Coaching Up practices suggested in the above questions need not be followed in their ideal form. A shared dinner hour, for instance, may not always be possible, because family circumstances and schedules vary considerably. Many families may not have the luxury of time or a tranquil environment in which to follow all these practices. The important point here is that it's still possible, with whatever time and resources you do have, to signal to a child your concern for his or her welfare and your faith in him or her. In the end it's not a question of the quantity of communicating you do but of the quality and care with which you build connection, provide support, and offer direction. Countless stories of kids overcoming even the harshest of backgrounds testify to the fact that there is no power in a child's life like a trusted, loving parent or other adult.

So, if you are not entirely happy with your answers to the six questions above, practice doing things differently. Introduce more warmth, more contact, and more connection into your daily interactions with your family members, and see what happens. A wonderful secret about practicing connection in these ways is this: it's highly contagious. When you forge authentic connections, they go deep—and are both reciprocal and enduring.

Providing Authentic Support

Back in the chapter devoted to this topic, I spent some time running through four effective forms of support:

- offering positive feedback, both directly and indirectly (that is, by reporting positive feedback you've heard from someone else)
- sharing a broader view by reminding the person you're coaching up that the present situation or issue is not the whole picture, that he or she will be growing, changing, learning, acquiring new skills, and so on
- removing obstacles in a person's path, for instance, making sure he or she has the tools needed for whatever interests he or she wants to pursue and the time and space to pursue them
- just being present, one-on-one, without necessarily saying a word

All these forms of support work just as well in families as they do in sports and business contexts. Here I'd just like to expand a bit on the importance of sharing a broader, more developmental and growth-oriented view, especially for younger kids.

Young kids really do live in the present moment. For some of us, awash in plans and lists and calendars full of meetings, living in the present moment is an aspiration! But for little kids, and even for adolescents, it can mean that every kind of unpleasantness feels doomed to last an eternity. They haven't yet grasped the reality that things happen and then other things happen, or that, generally, uncomfortable feelings fade and new, better feelings come along. It can be incredibly helpful not to dismiss their unhappy feeling but to acknowledge it and agree that it's crummy and even welcome their talking about how they feel at that moment, and then to assure them that tomorrow will be another day and they will very likely feel a whole lot better. This sounds so obvious, doesn't it? But even adults can lose sight of the possibility of happier days ahead.

One family I know posted on its refrigerator a list of things the kids would need to learn to be ready to go off into the world and have their own houses and families. The list looked something like this:

Things Kids Need to Learn to Do to Be Ready to Move Away from Home and Have Their Own Families

Brush teeth
Wash hands and face
Take a bath and wash hair
Cross the street safely
Use good table manners
Read a book
Write a story
Do arithmetic
Ride a bicycle

Swim
Take good care of a pet
Make healthy breakfasts, lunches, and dinners
Wash dishes
Sweep and vacuum floors
Wash floors
Clean bathrooms and kitchens
Rake leaves
Shovel snow
Use tools: hammer, screwdriver, paintbrush
Balance a checkbook
Pay bills
Drive a car

Every time the kids in the family saw that list, they were reminded that this business of being little and relatively powerless was not their ultimate destiny in life. In effect, their parents were helping the kids shift their perspective from a fixed mindset to a growth mindset. These concepts are presented and discussed fully in *Mindset: The New Psychology of Success*, by Carol Dweck, which I strongly recommend. Basically, a person with a fixed mindset believes that intelligence and ability are static, whereas a person with a growth mindset believes that intelligence and ability are developing qualities that can be transformed through hard work and determination.

As Carol Dweck says in her book, "Mindsets can be trained by the way we praise. We all want our children or employees to achieve great results, but to encourage the right behaviors in the longer term, it's important to create an environment that encourages hard work, effort, and growth. Praise effort and learning. Avoid praising results unless they are a byproduct of solid effort and lessons learned."

So a parent who wants to ensure that a child has a growth mindset will support the child by praising his or her commitment, effort, and improvement—not the resulting grades in school or number of hits or free throws. Big Ed Battier had that one right for sure. It's the growth mindset that counts. Another word for that willingness to pour effort into doing things well? It's called *character*. And don't we all want to encourage kids to build character?

Here's another suggestion for providing powerful support: if you haven't already done so, establish a tradition of formal family meetings. These can be a terrific way to reinforce the web of genuine connections within a family and to support individual family members. They're different from dinner table conversations because they have a strict format, and often they focus on a theme or issue. Some families like to hold such meetings on a regular schedule (e.g., weekly or monthly), while others prefer to call such meetings whenever any member of the family wants one. The meetings can be as brief or as long as they need to be for each person to be fully heard and respected. But they must be held sacred: no cell phones allowed, no distractions, and everyone present and attentive.

In my family, when I was growing up, when we held a family meeting we borrowed a tradition from Native American culture and used a Talking Stick. It was just an ordinary stick one of us had picked up somewhere, but it conveyed considerable authority. Whoever held the Talking Stick—even the youngest kid, who was always me—was entitled to speak, and the others listened respectfully, without interrupting. When the speaker finished saying whatever he or she thought and felt about the topic at hand, someone else could request the Talking Stick and either respond to the first person or say whatever he or she was thinking and feeling.

Family meetings can take place for all kinds of reasons. Maybe you want to involve everyone in planning a family vacation. Maybe there need to be an adjustment in the distribution of responsibilities for household chores. Or maybe one person is having a problem and welcomes advice about how to handle it. These meetings can be as lively, humorous, and happy making as any other get-together. Or they can be quite serious, as when a meeting is held to mourn a loss or struggle with an issue. The important thing is that everyone is present and committed to everyone else. When the meeting is called to focus on a problem one family member is having, the meeting can generate an amazing amount of multilateral support for that individual.

Coaching Up!

Finally, in the area of providing support, I want to mention a lesson I learned from the realm of dog training. This could be the most useful lesson I've learned from a trainer of any kind.

Not long ago, after growing up with family dogs, and after returning from living abroad for two years, I found myself finally in circumstances where it was possible to have a dog of my own. So I acquired a Rhodesian ridgeback puppy, whom I named DJ. As a puppy present, my mother gave DJ and me a series of puppy training classes with a top-notch trainer. The idea was not to train the puppy himself but to train the puppy's new owner, who in turn would train the puppy.

The trainer came to my house for our first session. At first he just observed DJ and me interacting for a while. Then he sat down and took DJ onto his lap, patting him and murmuring to him. After a minute or two he put DJ on his back, still holding him securely, and started moving his legs gently and inserting his fingers between the pads of his paws. Occasionally DJ would wiggle a little, looking uncomfortable, and I would get uncomfortable on his behalf and feel like grabbing him away from the trainer. But the trainer would immediately slip DJ a tiny bit of what turned out to be dried beef liver, and DJ would stop wiggling to enjoy it. And then the trainer would continue moving his legs around, and so on. This whole exercise lasted just a couple of minutes. Then the trainer put DJ back down on the floor and patted him approvingly.

I asked him what that exercise had been about. He explained that it's useful to think of puppies' brains as being basically binary. In every new situation, a puppy is assessing whether this new thing is good or bad, pleasant or unpleasant, okay or not okay.

People naturally want their puppies' whole lives to be pleasant, but unfortunately the world doesn't work that way. A puppy must get used to some situations—such as visits to the vet, for instance, or unfriendly older dogs at the dog park—that are decidedly unpleasant. The idea is to teach puppies that it's okay sometimes to go through temporary unpleasantness, because things will get better very soon. You do this by creating a very mild discomfort—making the puppy lie on his back in an unfamiliar lap, for instance, or asking him to sit still for a whole minute without moving before being released from that command—and while the puppy remains obediently in that situation, you sweeten the deal with periodic bursts of deliciously flavored treats. A puppy conditioned in this manner will likely be calmer and more resilient going into new experiences than a puppy for whom all new situations and minor discomforts trigger panic.

I'm making this little digression into the realm of canine psychology because the lesson it conveys seems so relevant to the principles underlying the Coaching Up Model. For a puppy, all situations are either positive—he or she is happy—or negative—he or she is anxious, uncomfortable, sad, scared, hungry, or whatever. In every new experience, the puppy's owner has the opportunity to add to the puppy's store of information about the world by either coaching him or her up or coaching him or her down.

And the same principle applies to human interactions generally. Even when we exchange the most routine greetings with each other, we can always ask ourselves, Did the other person come away from that exchange feeling more upbeat or less so? Have I been a good, useful, positive presence in that person's life today, or has my presence had the opposite effect?

What I'm suggesting here is that it may be useful to move through life with the assumption that there are very few truly neutral exchanges between human beings. We are all such exquisitely tuned instruments of communication that we are constantly sending and receiving thousands of subtle signals. We don't have to use little bits of dried beef liver, and in fact I'd advise against it. But wouldn't it be awesome if we all, in every interaction, put effort into coaching each other up?

Offering Concise Direction

As noted earlier, in our chapter on this dimension of the Coaching Up Model, once you have built a truly strong authentic connection and then underscored it by providing ample genuine support, your family members are very likely to be eager to listen to any concise direction you have to offer. Naturally, you will want to keep it brief and to the point.

And a final thought for this family chapter: if your concise direction to a child involves doing a chore of some kind, try, at least for the first few times the child does that chore, to join the child in doing it and to make a game of it. All chores are pleasanter when shared, and everyone likes a game.

My father has always been great at making games of chores. For instance, in New England, where I grew up, autumn meant that at some point all the leaves would fall off the trees, and my father would ask my sister and me to give him a hand raking them up.

Generally speaking, raking leaves wasn't much fun. I preferred all sorts of other ways to spend a Saturday afternoon, such as kicking a soccer ball around and playing video games with my friends. But I will admit that raking leaves with my dad and sister was really fun. The three of us would compete to see who could rake his or her leaves into the biggest pile, and then we would work together to stuff them into big biodegradable bags. The competition in raking was intense, and the teamwork in bagging the leaves was equally entertaining. Inevitably we would discover a few worms in the leaves (which I enjoyed, though my sister did not).

But the most fun came at the end of stuffing each bag: my dad would pick up my sister or me (we took turns) and stand us up on top of the open bag full of leaves, steadying us with a hand on each arm while we jumped up and down as forcefully as possible to pack the leaves down into the bag. Then, we would get off the bag and take turns running and belly flopping onto the bag to pack it down even more.

Now, that was fun! I felt like a World Wrestling Entertainment wrestler leaping from high on the ropes. To this day, when I see kids raking leaves, part of me still gets excited about the job.

As for my dad, he taught us some valuable lessons—about the joy in competition and teamwork, the satisfaction that comes with a job well done, and the environmental and economic value of using as few bags as possible (hence the need to put all that energy into packing down those leaves)—all while tiring us out and crossing a task off his list of household chores. And the cost of this lesson/fun activity was $0.

So, as a parent or other adult family member, you have almost infinite opportunities to create productive, win-win scenarios with the kids in your family, whereby you can teach them valuable life lessons. Most important, remember that every one of those opportunities tends to be binary: at all times, either you are coaching them up, or you're not. You may not be actively coaching them down, but if you just tell your kids to rake the leaves and come back when it's done, you're not coaching them up, either. You will have missed an opportunity to create real value for them by joining them in the chore and making a fun game of it.

So do yourself a favor, and take the Coaching Up Model to heart in your interactions with family members. Try it out for a couple of days, and see what happens. By consciously building authentic connections, providing genuine support, and offering concise direction to the people in your life, you will be enriching not only their lives, but your own.

7

Keeping It Real

"Regard your soldiers as children, and they may follow wherever you lead. Look upon them as your beloved sons and they will stand by you until death."

—Sun Tzu, *The Art of War*

In 1992 Bill Clinton won a town hall debate—and some would argue the entire U.S. presidential election—against presidential hopefuls George Bush and Ross Perot simply by *forming an authentic connection* with one voter, whom he did not previously know, with a direct, heartening, and strikingly real 30-second response to her question.

"How has the national debt personally affected each of your lives?" she asked of the three candidates. "And if it hasn't, how can you honestly find a cure for the economic problems of the common people, if you have no experience in what's ailing them?"

The woman asking the question was from a small town, and she and her friends had been hit hard by the recession. Perhaps she was also looking for an answer as to what each candidate would do, once in office, to improve the economy. But what she was really asking for was an authentic connection with the presidential candidates—men of significant means, who seemed to her very distant from her world of economic suffering. She also needed someone to offer genuine support for her and her friends, in a meaningful, heartfelt way. And yes, perhaps she hoped too for some sort of uplifting direction about how things could improve. Did the candidates understand what she was really looking for or what drove her to ask the question? We can judge their attentiveness to the real question, the sensitivity of their answers, and their ability to form authentic human relationships by how each candidate chose to answer.

Bush stumbled through an answer, eventually turning defensive, and argued that although he isn't personally directly affected by the recession or national debt, you don't have to be personally affected to understand that recessions are bad and painful for many people. To further illustrate this valid point, Bush said, "but I don't think it's fair to say, 'You haven't had cancer, so you don't know what it's like.'" Clearly, this is an example of a leader making a logically sound point, and backing it up with a good analogy, but completely missing the mark. He failed to address the woman's real concern because he was unable to understand or appreciate that the question was not important; what was important was the personal connection. He failed to so much as dip a toe into the pool of potential connection. As a result, he seemed even more distant from this voter, and the millions watching the debate at home, than he was when the debate started.

In Bush's answer there was no literal or figurative hand extended to touch the voter. Though the question was directed personally to each candidate, a charismatic leader should understand that the answer was not at all about what lowered interest rates their investments had suffered, how they'd had to sell one of their business holdings, or how they'd had visitors in their fancy offices who complained to them about the state of the economy and how that upset them. Instead, their goal in answering should have been to form an authentic connection with—and provide genuine support to—a member of the audience who was asking what so many voters at home wanted to ask as well: "Who are you guys? Are you real? Do you even get what's going on in this country? Do you know what it's like to fear being homeless, to not be able to provide groceries for your child? Do you get it?!? Are you listening to us, the real American people? Do you care about us at all?"

The point Bush made in his answer was not wrong. Of course we are all affected by recession and a crippling national debt, but some are affected much more harshly than others. And the question was about those people, the 95 percent. Who was asking the question? She was a single mother, struggling to make ends meet. She likely knew the cost of a gallon of milk. She counted every dollar. And she represented the vast majority of the American public in 1992.

So, how did Clinton so famously answer the question? In case you aren't familiar with this pivotal moment in presidential (and U.S.) history, here's what he did: before saying a word, he left the comfort of his podium and walked up to the edge of the stage, as close as he could get to the audience member who had asked the question— the closest he could get to reaching out and touching her—and paused before speaking. (You can see this in Seth Masket's YouTube video "Clinton vs. Bush in 1992 Debate.") Here's what he said (transcript by Sabrina

Siddiqui in "Bill Clinton Won 1992 Town Hall Debate by Engaging with One Voter"):

CLINTON: Tell me how it's affected you again.

QUESTIONER: Um—

CLINTON: You know people who've lost their jobs and lost their homes?

QUESTIONER: Well, yeah, uh-huh.

CLINTON: Well, I've been governor of a small state for 12 years. I'll tell you how it's affected me. Every year Congress and the president sign laws that make us do more things and gives (*sic*) us less money to do it with. I see people in my state, middle-class people—their taxes have gone up in Washington and their services have gone down while the wealthy have gotten tax cuts.

I have seen what's happened in this (*sic*) last four years when—in my state, when people lose their jobs there's a good chance I'll know them by their names. When a factory closes, I know the people who ran it. When the businesses go bankrupt, I know them.

And I've been out here for 13 months meeting in meetings just like this ever since October, with people like you all over America, people that have lost their jobs, lost their livelihood, lost their health insurance.

What I want you to understand is the national debt is not the only cause of that. It is because America has not invested in its people. It is because we have not grown. It is because we've had 12 years of trickle-down economics. We've gone from first to twelfth in the world in wages. We've had four years where we've produced no private-sector jobs. Most people are working harder for less money than they were making 10 years ago.

It is because we are in the grip of a failed economic theory. And this decision you're about to make better be about what kind of economic theory you want, not just people saying, "I'm going to go fix it" but what are we going to do? I think what we have to do is invest in American jobs, American education; control American health care costs; and bring the American people together again.

When Clinton returned to his podium, the message was clear; he was the candidate of the people, the candidate most in touch with regular Americans, and the candidate most likely, most driven, to do something to improve the situation. His words were good. But his understanding of what voters wanted to hear and how to connect with them emotionally and authentically and let them know that he not only is listening, but also actually *hears* them, enabled whatever policy agenda he offered in his concise direction in that debate, and in ensuing debates, to fall on ready ears among the voting public.

Furthermore, his words and his emotion behind the connection, support, and direction he offered were augmented by his perfect use of physical space and gestures. Let's review how Clinton's powerful response to the questioner paralleled the basic tenets of a Coaching Up Conversation, as we outlined it in Chapter 2.

If Possible, Choose the Setting for Maximum Comfort

Clinton left his podium at the back of the stage to walk to the edge of the audience so that he could be as close as possible to the voter (and to the cameras upon which millions of eyes around the country were fixed). This had the same effect as leaning in when your player is saying something important; shortening the physical space between you and your player screams, "I believe this is important, and I am intently listening."

Greet Your Player Warmly and Personally

Unlike Bush, Clinton did not jump right into his answer. He started with an informal request, "Tell me how it's affected you again." The voter was so stunned that he was asking her a question, rather than jumping into his answer, that she was at a loss for words.

Begin the Conversation with a Human Connection, Not a Functional One

Clinton then connected with her, personally and sympathetically: "you know people who've lost their jobs and lost their homes?" He asked one question and then another. With each question he reinforced that he cared and went even deeper, showing concern not just in his words, and not just in his physical closeness, but also in his voice. No one in the room could have doubted the sincerity of his words to follow.

Keep Your Posture Relaxed, and Speak Slowly, Clearly, and Thoughtfully

Clinton was by far the most relaxed candidate on the stage throughout the debate. Before he spoke, he paused to gather his thoughts. He paused in between thoughts to lick his lips and show that he was earnestly thinking. His hand gestures were casual but not informal. He spoke the way he would speak to a friend at a dinner table at a nice restaurant; that is, he was respectful of the space and setting, but at the same time comfortable in his own skin and very much hoping for every word to be clear and understood.

Stay Focused on Your Player

Whereas Bush looked around the room, taking his eyes off the voter, Clinton's eyes never swayed. He was locked in. This was about her, not about the room full of people or the other candidates on the stage. She had his undivided attention, as though nothing mattered more than his connection with her and support for her.

Practice Humor and Humility

While the seriousness of this particular situation would have made humor inappropriate, the candidates had a golden opportunity to present themselves humbly, in a situation in which humility was most needed. Bush, however, became defensive rather than humble. He moved to analogies to justify the logical soundness of his assertion that one can relate to another's circumstances without being in his or her shoes. In doing so, he only further positioned himself as someone squarely in the one percent.

Clinton, in contrast, embraced the opportunity to position himself as humble. This was not about him; this was about his people, the working-class people of Arkansas, and the millions like them around the country, who were suffering. He was their candidate, their humble elected official, raised in small-town rural America to go on to have this very moment to do something to help them, the people he calls friends, the people he knows, the people of whom (you could almost start to believe) he is one:

"Well, I've been governor of a small state for 12 years. I'll tell you how it's affected me. Every year Congress and the president sign laws that make us do more things and gives (*sic*) us less money to do it with. I see people in my state, middle-class people—their taxes have gone up in Washington and their services have gone down while the wealthy have gotten tax cuts.

"In my state, when people lose their jobs there's a good chance I'll know them by their names. When a factory closes, I know the people who ran it. When the businesses go bankrupt, I know them."

Like politicians, many coaches and business and community leaders often make the mistake of thinking that the substance of their words, or the details of their plan, are what is most important. Without forming an authentic connection with your players—whether they be athletes, employees, voters, family members, or friends—and without really listening, really hearing them, and then responding with genuine support, demonstrated through the whole of your body and your voice—no message will be truly heard and felt. As Jerry Lynch, PhD, describes in *Coaching with Heart*: "you will discover that by being a heart-directed leader, you will empower others and simultaneously, gain power yourself. Like electricity, the more energy and love you conduct, the more you receive. In truth you never need to display power. Others just feel it and respect it because such an extraordinary leader radiates and emanates personal power."

A Final Word

"I am the decisive element. It is my personal approach that creates the climate. . . . I possess tremendous power to make life miserable or joyous. . . . I can humiliate or humor, hurt or heal."

—attributed to both Johann Wolfgang
von Goethe and Haim Ginott

The corporate world has long looked to sports for inspirational analogies. We're all familiar with the clichés: "There is no *I* in *team*," "Practice makes perfect," "You miss every shot you don't take," and "Let's hit this one out of the ballpark." It makes sense that these and similar sayings have become commonplace across all kinds of work settings. After all, it's just as important in business as in sports for leaders to encourage colleagues to rally around a mission and work together (hard!) to drive results.

But the inspirational clichés are pretty superficial. I've written this book because I am convinced that there is a far deeper and more transformational lesson to be learned from the ways great coaches reach and inspire their players. The key insight is this: in the corporate world, as in the world of competitive sports, superb performance is all about relationships. The best coaches are simply, at bottom, the best, most inspirational relationship builders. They focus their time and energy on building authentic connections with their players, providing genuine support to them in good times and bad, and saving their direction for the end of each conversation and keeping it concise.

Above all, the best coaches are consistent. They maintain an even keel. They stand by their values and treat their players with respect and compassion, regardless of the score at the moment or whether they have a winning or losing record that season. And when they do put in their two cents' worth, they know how to keep their direction concise. Moreover, each player understands that the coach always has in mind the team's best interest—and therefore each player's ultimate best interest as well. The bottom line is that the coach strives, in everything he or she does, to coach every player up.

This book is meant to serve as a basic guide to a simple, straightforward, easy-to-learn method for more effective coaching. The Coaching Up Model boils down to these three essential elements:

1. Build an authentic connection
2. Provide genuine support
3. Offer concise direction

In any new relationship or first-time critical conversation, your first priority must be building the connection, followed by providing support, followed by offering concise direction. So, in the course of a 30-minute one-on-one conversation with a direct report, you may want to spend 15 minutes on connecting, 10 on supporting, and 5 on offering direction. If instead you spend 20 minutes putting forth direction after direction, you will have squandered time that should have been devoted to connecting with and supporting your player. Remember too that throughout these conversations, you want to spend at least as much time listening as talking.

Of course, when you have already built and solidified a long-established, fully trusting and transparent relationship with the other person, you may occasionally have conversations that start and end with direction. After all, one of the big benefits of practicing the Coaching Up Model is that, in the long run, it saves you time by enabling you to jump quickly into tackling pressing issues. But tread lightly here. If you move to a pattern of constant direction in all interactions, even with a player with whom you have succeeded in forging an authentic connection, you run the risk that over time you may erode the foundation of your relationship. You need to go back from time to time and check to ensure that the foundation of your relationship is still solid. It's good policy to periodically reinforce your connection, provide genuine support, and show your appreciation by recognizing the player both privately and publicly.

Authentic connection, genuine support, and concise direction—in that order. Not sometimes, not when it's convenient for you, not when you have free time in your day, but *all the time*. Even when it's hard. Even when it feels like you just don't have time for it. Remember this model when the clock is winding down; remember it in the middle of a fight; and remember it in the middle of a run at a championship season. Take a deep breath, and live by the model. And yes, live by it not only in a critical conversation with a direct report, but also in the heat of a major boardroom decision and in the comfort of your home, with people you love. Make it your mantra.

Trust the Coaching Up Model, live by it, and watch what happens all around you. Your relationships will flourish. As you coach people up, they will blossom and thrive, while you will become a more effective, more productive, and more fulfilled leader. People will choose to work *with* you precisely because they never feel they are working *for* you. In fact, if you lead well by practicing this model, you—and they—will feel that you are not managing them but serving them.

And they, in turn, may be inspired by your example to begin coaching other people up. Imagine what it would feel like to create an organization in which everyone, all the time, was forging authentic connections with one another, giving one another genuine support, and offering concise direction, up and down and across the organization—and even out to clients, suppliers, and others. Wouldn't that feel amazing?

I hope, as you put this book down, that you are feeling inspired to put the Coaching Up Model into active practice, starting today, right now. My wish is that through your actions, as much as your words, you will be modeling this model, to the great benefit of everyone in your organization and in your personal life. I hope you will find it both life changing, as I have, and richly rewarding.

Wishing you every success,

Jordan Fliegel

PS: If you have any questions about the Coaching Up Model, or any comments you'd like to offer, please reach out through my website, www.jordanfliegel.com. I'd love to hear how your experience with the model has helped you as a leader and what impact it has had on your colleagues and others close to you.

Bibliography and Suggested Reading

Chandler, Steve, and Scott Richardson. *100 Ways to Motivate Others: How Great Leaders Can Produce Insane Results Without Driving People Crazy.* 3rd ed. Pompton Plains, New Jersey: Career Press, 2012.

Dweck, Carol S. *Mindset: The New Psychology of Success.* Reprint ed. New York: Ballantine Books, 2007.

Ehrmann, Joe. *InSideOut Coaching: How Sports Can Transform Lives.* New York: Simon & Schuster, 2011.

Fliegel, Jordan Lancaster. *Reaching Another Level: How Private Coaching Transforms the Lives of Professional Athletes, Weekend Warriors, and the Kids Next Door.* Boston: CoachUp, Inc., 2014.

Goleman, Daniel. "What Makes a Leader?" In *HBR's 10 Must Reads on Emotional Intelligence*, 1–22. Edited by Harvard Business Review Press staff. Boston: Harvard Business Review Press, 2015.

Hacker, Gene, Barbara Hershey, and Dennis Hopper. *Hoosiers*, film. Directed by David Anspaugh. Beverly Hills: MGM Studios, 1986.

Kohn, Stephen E., and Vincent D. O'Connell. *9 Powerful Practices of Really Great Mentors: How to Inspire and Motivate Anyone*. Pompton Plains, New Jersey: Career Press, 2015.

Lynch, Jerry. *Coaching with Heart: Taoist Wisdom to Inspire, Empower, and Lead in Sports & Life*. Rutland, Vermont: Tuttle Publishing, 2013.

Masket, Seth."Clinton vs. Bush in 1992 Debate." YouTube video, 4:08. https://www.youtube.com/watch?v=7ffbFvKlWqE.

Patterson, Kerry, Joseph Grenny, Ron McMillan, and Al Switzler. *Crucial Conversations: Tools for Talking When Stakes Are High*, New York: McGraw-Hill, 2002.

Porath, Christine, and Christine Pearson. "The Price of Incivility: Lack of Respect Hurts Morale—and the Bottom Line." In *HBR's 10 Must Reads on Emotional Intelligence*, 93–104. Edited by Harvard Business Review Press staff. Boston: Harvard Business Review Press, 2015.

Siddiqui, Sabrina."Bill Clinton Won 1992 Town Hall Debate by Engaging with One Voter." *Huffington Post*, October 16, 2012. http://www.huffingtonpost.com/2012/10/16/bill-clinton-debate_n_1971685.html.

Tzu, Sun. *The Art of War*, Basic Books, 1994. Translated by Ralph D. Sawyer.

Weinschenk, Susan M. *How to Get People to Do Stuff: Master the Art and Science of Persuasion and Motivation.* San Francisco: New Riders, 2013.

Whitmore, John. *Coaching for Performance: GROWing Human Potential and Purpose: The Principles and Practice of Coaching and Leadership.* 4th ed. London: Nicholas Brealey Publishing, 2009.

Zenger, John H., Joseph R. Folkman, and Scott K. Edinger. *The Inspiring Leader: Unlocking the Secrets of How Extraordinary Leaders Motivate.* New York: McGraw-Hill Education, 2009.

Zenger, John H., and Kathleen Stinnett. *The Extraordinary Coach: How the Best Leaders Help Others Grow.* New York: McGraw-Hill Education, 2010.

Acknowledgments

Great thanks first to Lia Ottaviano for encouraging me to write this book and to Lauren Freestone for her terrific production assistance.

Many thanks also to the entire team at CoachUp who helped me in this undertaking, especially all the CoachUp coaches who spent hours sharing their insights with me and contributing to our surveys; and special thanks to Grant Covington, who put those surveys together.

To all my coaches over the years—from my youth to the professional teams I played on—thank you from the bottom of my heart for all your patience and support. This book is a direct reflection of your effect on my life. In particular, I would like to thank my college basketball head coach, Tim Gilbride; you've always put your players first. To my long-time private coach, Greg Kristof, thanks for teaching me how to be disciplined and efficient on and off the court; without your coaching I would never have made it as a high school varsity player, much less enjoyed all the benefits that my eventual sports career brought me. Finally, to my boxing trainer and good friend, Tommy Duquette, thank you for being a true Zen master of the ring. I've learned so much from you, and I look forward to having you in my corner for years to come.

To Shane Battier, world-class team player, leader, family man, and friend, thank you for being such a source of inspiration to me and to so many others. Sincere thanks also for contributing the hard-won wisdom in your powerful foreword to this book.

Along with the genes for height, my parents also bestowed on me, for better or worse, the desire to try my hand at writing. Thanks to both of you for your encouragement and help with this book.

To my father, Dorian Fliegel, thank you for helping me boil down what I'm trying to say to its essential meaning. As you have done throughout my life, Dad, you helped me focus on what truly matters, and for that I am forever grateful.

Last, but most certainly not least, a huge thank you to my mother, Kathleen Lancaster, without whom this book would still be in my head rather than on paper. What I enjoyed most about the process of writing this book was the excuse it provided to spend even more time with you. I can't imagine a better writing partner. I love you, Mom.

About the Author

Jordan Fliegel is an entrepreneur, startup investor and advisor, and author. He is the founder of CoachUp, Inc., America's leading sports coaching company, whose online service connects athletes of all ages with private coaches to help them reach the next level in sports and life. As this book goes to press in 2016, CoachUp has more than 20,000 coaches across the United States conducting thousands of training sessions every week in some 25 sports. CoachUp has attracted more than $15 million in venture funding and has won numerous awards, as well as celebrity endorsements from NBA MVP and world champion Stephen Curry and NFL star Julian Edelman. In addition, CoachUp has been featured hundreds of times on television and in the press, in outlets such as *Live with Kelly and Michael*, *Late Night with Seth Meyers*, Fox News, *The Wall Street Journal*, *The New York Times*, *Forbes*, and *USA Today*.

Within the startup ecosystem, Jordan plays several active roles: as an early stage technology investor in more than 40 startups through Bridge Boys, a seed fund he cofounded in 2012; as an advisor to numerous venture-backed startups; and as a mentor at top incubators, such as Techstars Boston and Mass Challenge. In 2014 he was named to the *Boston Business Journal* 40 Under 40 list, and in 2015 he was named to the prestigious *Inc.* 30 Under 30 list and was a finalist for Ernst & Young's New England Entrepreneur of the Year.

A frequent guest columnist at *Inc.* on the topics of entrepreneurship, coaching, and leadership, Jordan published his first book, *Reaching Another Level: How Private Coaching Transforms the Lives of Professional Athletes, Weekend Warriors, and the Kids Next Door*, in 2014. A sought-after public speaker, he has lectured and participated in panels on entrepreneurship, venture capital financing, and leadership at numerous business forums, including the Harvard Business School and the Massachusetts Institute of Technology (MIT) Sloan School of Management.

Before launching his entrepreneurial career, Jordan played professional basketball in Israel. He holds a BA from Bowdoin College with a double major in government and philosophy, as well as an MBA from Tel Aviv University. Learn more at JordanFliegel.com or follow him on Twitter @jordanfliegel.

About His Collaborator

Kathleen Landis Lancaster has pursued a long career as a senior writer with global management consultancies: first with Arthur D. Little, Inc., where she ultimately served as Vice President for Corporate Communications worldwide, and subsequently with the Boston Consulting Group. Earlier she enjoyed some spirited years as a Peace Corps Volunteer in Bahia, Brazil; a fashion model in New York City and Paris; an editorial assistant with the *Atlantic* and Houghton Mifflin; a Boston-based freelance journalist; and a restaurant critic for *Bostaston* magazine. She holds a BA from Smith College in philosophy, Phi Beta Kappa and magna cum laude, and a professional chef's certificate from Madeleine Kamman's school, the Modern Gourmet. The devoted mother of two amazing adults, one of whom is the author of this book, she lives with her husband, Michael Keating, and their dogs in Cambridge, Massachusetts, where she delights in collaborating with inspiring authors as their scribe, thought partner, editor-in-chief, and muse.

Index

160   *Index*

concise direction
  (*continued*)
  example, 76–81
  for family, 124–127
  offering, 85–88
  overview, xiv, 17,
    18–21, 73,
    75–76
  for transformational
    leadership, 82–85
  transparent leadership
    for, 81–82
  verbose direction *versus*,
    20
confidence building,
  36–37, 62
connection. *See* authentic
  connection
consistency, 143–144
criticism, problem of,
  70–72
Crucial Conversations
  (Patterson, Grenny,
  McMillan, Switzler),
  103
cultural differences,
  for greeting,
  42–43

D
"dap" (informal
  handshake), 44
Detroit Country Day
  School, xxii, xxxiii
direct concise direction, 85
direction. *See* concise
  direction
dog training example,
  122–124
dress code, 100–101
Duke University,
  xxii–xxxi, xxxiv
Duquette, Tommy, 14–21
Dweck, Carol, 119–120

E
Edinger, Scott K., 62, 89
Ehrmann, Joe, 9, 25
80/20 rule (Pareto
  Principle), 94–97
England, Chip, xxviii–xxx
exploratory conversation,
  98
Extraordinary Coach, The
  (Zenger, Stinnett), 5,
  50, 59, 84–85
eye contact, xxv, 51

168   *Index*

Washington, Deron, 79–80

Weinschenk, Susan, 9, 39, 51

Whitmore, John, 89–90

See also leadership; players

Y

Yellowjackets (Detroit Country Day School), xxii

Z

Zenger, John, 5, 50, 59, 62, 84–85, 89, 102